R. M'D Stirling

Inveresk Parish Lore From Pagan Times

R. M'D Stirling

Inveresk Parish Lore From Pagan Times

ISBN/EAN: 9783337428631

Printed in Europe, USA, Canada, Australia, Japan

Cover: Foto ©Thomas Meinert / pixelio.de

More available books at **www.hansebooks.com**

INVERESK

PARISH LORE

FROM

PAGAN TIMES.

BY

R. McD. STIRLING.

MUSSELBURGH:
PRINTED BY T. C. BLAIR.

1894.

YE BUKE

OF YE

PAROCHE AND KYRK

OF

INNERASK,

MWSKYLBRUCHSCHYRE

DEDICAT TO

YE PAROCHINARIS.

INTRODUCTION.

THE story of bygone times in small communities affords an admirable insight into the manners, customs, and social condition of the Scottish people.

A study of these old-world ways as they existed at Inveresk has yielded much delight to the author, and in response to frequent invitations he now offers some of the fruit he has gathered as a contribution to local history, not without hope that others may find in it some of the interest and pleasure he has experienced. Access to Parish and Burgh Records has enabled him to embody many facts never before published, and an endeavour has been made to convey an idea of how valuable these Records are.

In the compilation of the present work numerous and scarce publications in the Advocates' and other libraries have been consulted, and information kindly communicated by personal friends is here gratefully acknowledged.

CONTENTS.

CHAPTER.	PAGE.
I. Topographical,	1
II. Prehistoric,	12
III. Coming of the Romans,	20
IV. After the Romans,	29
V. Relics of the Romans,	36
VI. St. Michael's of Inveresk,	50
VII. Time of Wallace and Bruce,	67
VIII. Dawn of the Reformation,	79
IX. Reformation Period,	84
X. Ministry of Mr. Adam Colt,	90
XI. Old Communion Cups,	117
XII. Seventeenth Century Records,	127
XIII. Parish Finance—XVII. Century,	146
XIV. Close of XVII. Century,	154
XV. Opening of XVIII. Century,	160
XVI. Gloom followed by Sunshine,	168
XVII. Ministry of Dr. Carlyle,	175
XVIII. The Present Parish Church,	182
XIX. Dr. Moodie's and Mr. Beveridge's Ministries,	188
XX. Memorable Events,	196
XXI. Distinguished Parishioners,	203
XXII. Miscellanea,	214

ILLUSTRATIONS.

                                                                     PAGE.

1. Portrait of Author—Facing title page.
2. Communion Token, 1727—Back of title page
3. Old St. Michael's, Inveresk—Facing Chap. I.
   From Original Water Colour Drawing taken in 1803, the property of Admiral of the Fleet, Sir Alex. Milne, Bart., G.C.B.
4. Communion Token, 1841—Back of alternative title page.
5. Inveresk Church, 1805—S. W. View, . . 16
6. Oldest Minute Book, 1651, . . . 32
7. Pinkie House, General Sir Wm. Hope, Bart., C.B., 48
8. Fac-simile half-page Account Book, 1655, . 64
9. Rev. Adam Colt, M.A., . . 80
   From Portrait by Jameson at Gartsherrie House.
10. Inveresk House, J. A. Park, Esq., . . 96
11. Old Communion Plate, Charter Chest and Records, 112
12. Crest of Earl of Dunfermline—Page 117, . 128
13. Memorial Stone, Carberry Hill, where Queen Mary surrendered to the confederate Lords, 144
14. Monument of William Smyth, Town Clerk, . 160
    Stone Buried 1805, Recovered 1894.
15. Rev. Alexander Carlyle, D.D., . . 176
16. West End High Street, Musselburgh, . . 192
    Showing old house in which Commissioner Cardonnel received Smollett the Novelist, now removed.
17. Specimens of New Communion Plate, . . 208
18. Bit of Old Fisherrow, North Side, High Street, . 224
    Site now occupied with modern tenement.

Old St Michael's.

Chapter I.

TOPOGRAPHICAL.

INVERESK is an ancient and historic parish in the north-east of the county of Mid-Lothian. The burgh of Musselburgh forms part of it. Until early in the eighteenth century it was called Innerask and Musselburgh, but this conjunct designation has since then been dropped.

The parish is about three miles from north to south, and from two to two and a-half from east to west. Its northern boundary is the shore of the Firth of Forth from Ravenshaugh burn on the east to Magdalen burn on the west. The parishes of Duddingston, Newton, and Liberton in Mid-Lothian adjoin it on the west, Dalkeith and Cranstoun in the same county on the south, and Tranent and Prestonpans in Haddingtonshire on the east.

The Esk divides the parish into two nearly equal parts from south to north, and empties itself here into the Firth. The name Inveresk is significant of that position, and in itself contains evidence of antiquity. With a like geographical meaning similar compound place-names are common enough, but few indeed can tell as much as this one does. *Esk* comes out of a very old stock. Variations of it are found in Ax, Ex, Ox, Ux, Ouse, Uisque, Usk, Esce, all meaning water, and in many of these forms it is applied to rivers in Great Britain. Such root words, descriptive of the natural features of a country, *i.e.*, rivers, mountains and the like, cling with firm hold in common speech, while names given to places of abode are more subject to change when people of a different language become occupants. The importance of word study is coming more and more to be recognised. The very form of the word Inveresk helps to discover its history. It has been found that in words in use in Celtic times the descriptive part comes after the root portion; in those of Anglic or Saxon origin the reverse holds good. We are thus enabled to fix the period to which Inveresk belongs, and to trace it to the time of the Angles. Escemuthe, the name by which the earliest of the Saxon invaders knew it, is unquestionably Celtic. Esk, Eskmouth, Carberry (Caerbarren) have come down from the aboriginal Britons whom the Romans encountered. According to a recent writer on the subject of place-names, Musselburgh in its original form, signified "the fenced town of the Picts." When thus examined, the names of parish and burgh are, in themselves, charters of an antiquity sufficiently remote to

TOPOGRAPHY.

gratify the most exacting, and with which parishioner and burgess may feel proudly content.

As an example of the intuitive or traditional hold which successive generations retain of the original meaning of a very old word, it may be mentioned that nothing was more common half-a-century ago than to hear people in the parish speak of the Esk as the "watter." Nor was this a mere localism, as the writer thus discovered. When a small boy he enjoyed a jaunt to a pretty Tweedside Town. On asking for some water, the request was met with the query, "Waeter-waeter or well-waeter?" That is to say, was river water or pump water, water to wash in or water to drink wanted? River water was thus waeter-waeter, where the waeter was said to wax and to wane; and the same root idea was presented to the mind within sight of the Cheviots on the banks of the Tweed as within sight of the Pentlands on the banks of the Esk. To return to descriptive details, it may be pointed out that at the confluence of the Esk with the estuary, the Firth of Forth reaches its most southerly limit and its greatest width. The distance across is more than three times what it is between Granton and Burntisland, and fully eight times greater than where the Forth Bridge joins the two shores. What secondary causes have combined to scoop out the large elliptical bay that extends from Hound Point to Gullane, is a subject beyond the scope of this work. That glacial action had some share in the work, the presence of huge boulders upon the foreshore indicates. Whatever forces were employed, the Esk must have proved a counter-active. The tendency of rivers is to accumulate the soil they bear seawards near their mouths, and to cause the land to encroach on the sea. The present influence of the stream affords no index of the power it formerly had, and gives but a faint idea of its energy when it ran a broad, deep and rapid river before its sources were impounded for district supply.

The bay of Musselburgh furnishes shelter and good anchorage, and is much frequented by shipping when a storm rages in the North Sea or an easterly gale drives up the Firth.

The surface of the parish next the coast and near the river is comparatively flat, but rises to an elevation of 514 feet at Carberry Hill. Next the shore is the burghal portion which competent authorities consider to be an upraised sea level. It is fan shaped, the pivot point being at the parish church. For a considerable distance along the beach on either side of the mouth of the Esk, there is extensive links, which in England would be called downs. Dr. Carlyle writes in his article upon the parish in Sir John Sinclair's Statistical Account of Scotland, that every burgess of Musselburgh had a right of pasturage on the links. When such individual privileges came no longer to be permitted, this pasturage, which still formed part of the common good of the burgh, was until comparatively recently rouped annually. From time immemorial the links have been used as recreation ground by the inhabitants, but that portion to the east of the river is most widely known from being the golfing green and race course with which the name of the burgh is associated. At the time the present parish church was built, Musselburgh links was used as a military camp and drill ground. Later on, troops returned from the seat of war were sent here to recruit; and the value of the station as a sanatorium came to be so fully recognised that, when the British Army was reduced to a peace establishment after the battle of Waterloo, the cavalry barracks would have been erected at Musselburgh instead of at Piershill, but for some local obstacles that intervened.

Portions of the old sea margin which runs parallel to the south shore of the Firth can be traced crossing the parish. Upon one part of this elevation the Parish Church and village of Inveresk are situated. Its strategic importance at this point was so evident that the Romans established upon it an important station, which will be noticed in its proper place.

In the able treatise on "Traces of Ancient Water

Lines in Scotland," by the late Mr. David Milne Home, we find the following notice of the old sea margin just referred to: "At Musselburgh, a bank more or less steep, can be traced from Joppa, south of Portobello, crossing Magdalene Burn, New Hailes policy, the river Esk, the fields north of Inveresk Church, the grounds of Inveresk House, eastward by Pinkie Burn, and as far as Drummore Lodge at the east end of Musselburgh Links. The base of the bank is about 28 feet above high water. At Newbigging, the bank is distant about one and a-half miles from the existing shore. It is cut through by the Magdalene Burn, the river Esk and also by Pinkie Burn. This bank is in the boulder clay. It seems probable that, when the sea stood at the above level of 28 feet, the river Esk did not follow its present course to the sea, west of Inveresk Church, where there is now a vertical cliff. If that passage near Monkton village, Monktonhall, were blocked, a great lake would be formed, whose west margin would coincide with the long ridge of gravel running north from *Camp-end*, properly *Kaimend*, and the overflow of the lake would be by the small valley at Pinkie Burn situated to the east of Inveresk."

Elsewhere, in the same volume, Mr. Milne Home shows how closely the height above high water of this bank at Inveresk approximates to similar levels at other points on the shore of the Firth, and gives reasons for concluding that the present reduced area and lower level of the estuary had been reached before the time of the Roman occupation.

The soil of the parish ranges from light sandy loam to heavy and clayey land. It is generally fertile and productive, and is highly cultivated. The most approved methods of modern husbandry are followed, and the implements employed are of the most recent construction. Dr. Carlyle, the Parish Minister of Inveresk during nearly the whole of the latter half of last century, may be claimed to have been the first to give an impetus to the improvement which has since made steady progress. Down to the doctor's time the heavy lumbering ox plough continued to be used, and required not only a ploughman but a driver to manage the yoke. An ingenious blacksmith in Dalkeith, having constructed one of an improved type which a pair of horses could draw and a single man handle, Dr. Carlyle was shrewd enough to perceive its value, and at once employed it upon a farm he held. His neighbour, the Rev. Dr. Grieve of Dalkeith, did the same. The farmers round about laughed at this departure from use and wont, and doubtless cracked many a joke at the parsons' expense at their market-day meetings. But Jupiter lets us into the secret of his own and his friend's faith:—"They were acquainted with the practice of the ancients in this particular;" and, when the second year's crops under the new method came to be reaped, the increased yield and improved quality proved the men of the manse to be right, and the auld wives of the mains to be wrong.

Between the present condition of agriculture and its state last century the distance is immense. In 1760, the rental of land was 20/- to 25/- per acre, and up till then no bread but oat-cakes were the daily fare of working people. A ploughman's weekly wage was 5/-, and as the necessaries of life occasionally touched famine prices the pinch at times must have been hard indeed. About the year just mentioned, "some 700 acres in the fields of Inveresk" were divided among the neighbouring lairds and afterwards enclosed. The Howe Mire, part of the battlefield of Pinkie, had been previously a stagnant morass with ague and fever prevalent around it. Now, no portion of the parish is more healthy or yields better crops. *The lave*, as well as the lairds, have therefore been sharers in the gain.

The parish is well furnished with growing timber. Much planted last century has attained considerable size. Some of it is deserving of special notice. In the Duke of Buccleuch's policies, there are several fine specimens of the cedars of Lebanon near the Smeaton Entrance Lodge, and at another part are a number of very venerable oak trees, believed to be a remnant of the once extensive forest which extended from Craigmillar to the Esk, in the days when the Scottish Kings found in it a favourite hunting ground.

The air is pure, the climate healthy and the death rate low. After a long struggle with the timid, who dread any departure from what they have been accustomed to, and with those self-constituted guardians of public interests, who oppose every measure that involves outlay however beneficial, the advocates of progress prevailed, and a water supply and drainage system, properly constructed footpaths and carriage ways were secured. As a result, the sanitary condition has been advanced, and unsavoury dwellings are in the way of becoming a thing of the past. With an increasing attention to cleanliness,—personal, domestic and local,—and the supervision of properly qualified and energetic officials, the reputation of the locality, as a desirable place of residence, promises to become more conspicuous, and it is hoped it will rightfully take its place among the most popular of Scottish health resorts. Already capital has been attracted towards it for the erection of dwelling-houses of a superior class, and the manner in which these have been taken up proves that the investment will yield a fair return.

For situation and surroundings there are few places the parish need envy. Its old minister, Dr. Carlyle, claimed it to be " one of the most beautiful in Scotland," and he was not a man given to vapouring. Thomas Carlyle—uncompromising, hard headed and plain-speaking—is every bit as complimentary. In his elucidation of one of Cromwell's Musselburgh letters this occurs:—" We march, with defiant circumstance of war, round all accessible sides of Edinburgh; encamp on the Pentlands, return to Musselburgh for provisions; go to the Pentlands again—enjoy one of the beautifulest prospects, over deep-blue seas, over yellow cornfields, dusky Highland mountains, from Ben Lomond round to the Bass again."

Those who have visited the most famous sights in Europe have looked upon these same panoramic and historic scenes with admiration: others who have made acquaintance with the choicest landscapes of the West have been no less enamoured by them. Here the eye passes from Craigmillar, where Queen Mary stayed, to Carberry, where she surrendered; from the battlefield of Pinkie, where the Scots were routed, to that of Prestonpans where Charlie won; from the fortalice of Fa'side to the tower of Preston; from the fourteenth century turrets of Pinkie to the four hundred year old Clock Steeple of Musselburgh. Otherwise the view takes in the Pentlands and the Moorfoots, the Lammermoors and the Garletons, with North Berwick Law and the Bass like solitary sentinels on out-post duty. From the

German Ocean and Isle of May the sweep of the vision embraces the waters of the Firth, reflecting the wing-like canvas of sailing-craft, and streaked with the dusky trail of steamers' smoke. It steals along over the fair fields and busy towns dotted upon the Fifeshire Coast from Earlsferry to Kinghorn, from Inchkeith to Leith, from Arthur's Seat to Aberdour, from the woods of Dalmeny to the summit of Dumyat. Under exceptional conditions the higher summits of the Perthshire Grampians that rise above Strathmore are seen to overtop the nearer ranges in Fife and Forfar; and Ben Lomond, Ben Ledi and Ben Voirlich stand out clear and distinguishable against the evening sky. If within the compass of this horizon the eye may enjoy a perpetual feast, the mind becomes a participant in the pleasure when memory recalls the royal cavalcades, the processions of mitred dignitaries, the state welcomes, the military spectacles, the gorgeous funerals, the gay, splendid, solemn, sad history-making events that the parish has witnessed.

Chapter II.

PREHISTORIC.

A DOZEN years ago, anything known of human life in the parish before the commencement of the Christian era, was in the main conjectural. With the dawn of record the story began, but from the darkness beyond, light has since come, and the barrier previously impenetrable, has been partially unclosed. What the written page was searched for in vain, memorials of man found in the soil have revealed.

At Magdalen Bridge, close to the north-western boundary of the parish, a series of nine funereal urns were found about ten years since, in the strata of sand and gravel which immediately underlays the surface. These are preserved in the National Antiquarian Museum, Edinburgh. In one of these urns, a finely ornamented thin oval bronze blade was obtained, which placed their belonging to the bronze period beyond question. The discovery was looked upon as one of considerable importance, but it has been completely eclipsed by another more recently made at Kirk Park, immediately at the base of the eminence on which the church and church-yard are situated. To meet a demand for sand suitable for building purposes, the late Bailie George Lowe had his field opened up, and in the same strata as that at Magdalen Bridge, a number of stone cists with human remains have been found. Six years ago a single urn containing calcined human bones was come upon, and it was sent to the Antiquarian Museum. Till the summer of 1893 the excavation proceeded without further discovery, but then no fewer than eighteen urns were disinterred. All these, excepting three which were hopelessly broken in the handling, were acquired by the Queen's Remembrancer and are placed in the National Collection. There can be little doubt, the cemetery thus discovered was one of a remote antiquity, possibly an already forgotten one long before the first centuries of the Christian era. The collection of urns obtained in it includes the largest and smallest specimens acquired by the Museum, and it is particularly rich in examples of those tiny funereal vessels pierced with holes, which, in the absence of any certain knowledge of their purpose, have by some been called incense cups. Several of the urns have the simple punctured interlinear ornamentation peculiar to the Bronze period neatly carried round them, while one of the smaller held the cremated bones of an infant not more than three or four months old. Although it may be impossible to fix the exact date when these interments took place, one of the best qualified to form an opinion assigns them to a period not less than 600 B.C.

Following the view taken by this expert, a colony is seen to have been settled in the parish five and twenty centuries ago; and if it be granted that the remains contained in the cists and urns unearthed are probably those of its more important members only, then its numbers may be reckoned to have been all the larger.

Of those whose dwellings nestled and whose remains have thus been found it is possible to learn something, from what has been ascertained to be characteristic of the era in which they lived. This little community may be considered to have its counterpart in an Indian wigwam or in the village life of Central Africa at the present day. It was, however, advanced beyond the state of primitive man. Already it had learned that in a settled abode, greater security was to be obtained than fell to the lot of the isolated and migratory who lead a nomad life. In some of the industries progress had also been made. Their knowledge of the potter's art had, doubtless, come down from ancestors who had brought it with them when the British Isles still formed part of the continent of Europe. The form and finish given to the earthenware vessels already described, when put in comparison with others belonging to the Stone period, show a considerable advance, the latter being less shapely and sun-dried,—not fire-baked. For food supplies they would depend mainly upon hunting and fishing and such edible plants as they could find.

But what of their mental condition, what of them as thinking men? Surely the methods taken to preserve the bones of their departed and the articles sometimes put in the tomb beside them appear to suggest that they had some idea of a hereafter, and that their conception was no longer content with looking for it to be simply a happy hunting ground. A nobler belief seems to have begun to make way among them, an anticipation of good things desired, but denied;—rest and peace in place of toil and war. Faint and feeble that anticipation may have been, but if symbolism has any meaning they appear to have hoped that the sword, which had been often handled to defend or defy, would no longer be required, and its fragments therefore find their place in the funereal urn.

With these ancient Britons, years passed as they do still. To gladness and gloom, mirth and sadness, care and toil, they were no strangers. On the rain-cloud they saw God's bow pencilled, and, perchance even to their untutored minds it was not without a message. Such is a glimpse of the early colony at this spot which recent discoveries have given.

But to a far higher past the mind is led by another discovery made at Olive Bank about eleven years since. In the strata already mentioned, a couple of large oak trees were found embedded at a considerable depth, not fossilized, but sound and serviceable. The novelty of the find procured for it prominence and publicity. Before removal, the trees were examined *in situ* by distinguished geologists and archæologists. Such questions as whence and how they had come, and how long they had remained there were carefully considered. The result assigned them to a period 6,000 years ago.

Two noble mantelpieces were made from one of them, and with a plank of the timber, formed an attractive group in the Forestry Exhibition, Edinburgh, 1884. The catalogue entry reads:—"One Dining-room and one Hall Mantelpiece, and one plank from an Oak tree of great age, probably at or about the time when Neolithic Man entered Britain."

Veritable vestiges of creation, it may with some confidence be affirmed, these trees did not fall where they were found, for they had a deep layer of pure sand below as well as above them. Nor had they been the victims of decay. Most likely they had either been uprooted by a hurricane or a flood, and had been transported on the bosom of the waters to the spot where they were found.

INVERESK CHURCH, 1805.

Back through the long milleniums the mind may strain and peer, contemplate the planting of the acorns from which these giants of the forest sprung, watch them shoot up as tender saplings on through many years of luxuriant growth, and see in it all those very forces at work by which the Creator still accomplishes his purpose and fulfils his plan.

A retrospective survey of six thousand years looks large and long when considered by itself, or if measured by the span of a life-time or the changes of a century. Put, however, in comparison with geologic periods, its comparative magnitude is completely altered. The record of the rocks back even to the relatively recent carboniferous formations opens out a far wider view, and the story which it tells can here be read. Coal has been worked in the parish for nearly seven centuries. Between the years 1202 and 1218, the monks of Newbattle obtained right to work coal and stone on their lands of Preston,—*i.e.* Priesttown,—westward to Pinkie Burn, by charter from Seyer d'Quincy, Lord of the Manor of Tranent. Peat must also have been obtainable, for there occurs an entry in the chartulary of Kelso Abbey giving right to cast it at Easter Duddingston, to one Reginald d'Bosco, and faggots of course would be found in the neighbouring forest.

The coal field in Inveresk parish is part of the

great Lothian coal basin, which geologists say is of an older formation than that in Durham and Northumberland.

No fewer than forty seams are met with in the coal measures of the Lothians, and these vary from two-and-a-half to nine feet in thickness. The article "Inveresk" in the New Statistical Account, written in 1839 by the late Rev. J. G. Beveridge, contains interesting particulars of its geological features. In that admirably compiled descriptive notice, six collieries are mentioned, three at work, three recently before discontinued. The former were at New Craighall, Monktonhall, and Edmonston, the latter had been at Pinkie Burn, Midfield and Cowpits. All have been long closed. The withdrawal from so many workings is not due to the supply having been exhausted, but to the difficulty and expense of reaching the lower seams having become greater than the enterprise could bear. In the endeavour made to cope with the difficulties presented, a great pumping engine was put down at the New Craighall pit that at the time was reckoned a marvel of its kind. Of so great an interest was it the subject among engineering circles at home and abroad, that an elaborate account of it was published in book form, about sixty years since, unique in this respect, that while one page was printed in English the other facing it was given in corresponding French. The remains of the engine-house still stand in a field on Stoney-hill farm near Newhailes Station.

In all the coal pits already mentioned, and in those afterwards opened at Wallyford and Carberry, animal and vegetable remains have been frequently found. The existence of this great accumulation of carboniferous strata tells of a time when the climate was tropical and vegetation dense. On the other hand some of the fossils it contains, indicate an alternative aquatic condition necessary for their existence, and countenance the supposed presence of a great lake or sea, the denizens of which belonged to species no longer met with either in salt or fresh water.

Chapter III.

COMING OF THE ROMANS.

MORE than half-a-century before the beginning of the Christian era, Julius Cæsar effected a landing in the south of Britain; and from the day he planted his standards upon her shores Britannia assumed a fresh importance. "Trade followed the flag" even then, and a conquest by many reckoned worthless proved to be valuable. Before the end of the second century, barren Britain had become an exporting country, and was looked to for supplies of cattle, corn, etc., by the continent. But the Roman generals and the legions they commanded found it no child's play to establish the Imperial power and make it respected. The native races were hardy and brave, and many a well-contested battle had to be won before they yielded to the rule of the conqueror. Time was thus occupied, and it was not till Julius Cæsar had been replaced by Julius Agricola that, somewhere about A.D., 80, the Roman troops penetrated into North Britain. These were not the days of electric telegraphs or military intelligence departments. Wheatstone or Von Moltke had not yet arisen. But even as news speeds over the plains of India or tidings of a plentiful supply at market reach the costermongers of London with marvellous rapidity and by means inexplicable, so, doubtless, tidings of an enemy in the land would reach the little community on the banks of the Esk at Musselburgh. Notwithstanding, in the meantime food would require to be obtained and the pot kept boiling as best they could. By-and-bye, like the mutterings of a coming storm, the news would be repeated. The stories of strife and struggle begin to come in more detail, and fugitives from the fight picture its horrors. Suddenly danger is at the door. A strange glittering mass is descried pouring over the height at Carberry, and on it the sunbeams flash and sparkle. What can it be? Nothing else than the brass helmets, polished armour and glittering weapons of the approaching foe. What is to be done? Time is precious but it is short. Hurriedly they prepare to defend their dwellings, and if need be sacrifice themselves for home's sake. These heroes of the hamlet are brave, but they are undisciplined, and neither in numbers nor in equipment have any chance against their assailants. Nearer the legionaries come with the steady tramp and soldiery bearing, and well-knit frames of men inured to discipline and danger. The orders of the centurions ring clearly out, a change of formation is made, and the two forces stand face to face in deadly conflict. The fight does not last long, but it is not ended till many a wound has been given, many a life lost, and victory won by the invader.

The troops of the Mistress of the World thus came to the shore of Bodotria—Sinus Orientalis—the Firth of Forth, displayed her eagles and established her rule, where we now call Inveresk. Whether our ancestors who were worsted in this fight had time to put on their war paint and turn out in review order history neglects to say. We know they were fond to do so, and need have no scruple in supposing they felt quite as important in their own estimation as any soldier who ever donned a uniform, when they had their persons bedaubed. Like the Chinese who encountered the British troops with a mighty din of drums and with banners bearing frightful monsters painted on them, these Britons doubtless vainly fancied their woaded bodies would scare off an enemy. Anyhow, this practice obtained for them the name by which they are now mostly known, viz.:—Picts, that is painted, of which we are reminded by the word depict.

The movement forward to Inveresk carried the great Roman road known as Watling Street from coast to coast along the island. From Dover it led to London and on to Chester. Reference to

a map shows that a line nearly due north from
Chester, indicates pretty nearly the course it took
by way of Carlisle, across the Cheviots, by Jedburgh, Melrose, Gala Water, Borthwick and Vogrie
to Inveresk.

Once settled in their new station these sons of
Mars must have looked across upon the hills of
Fife with some degree of awe. Strange stories
were told them of the unknown land beyond. Its
air was said to be so poisonous that whoever
entered it died. Reserved to be the abode of
departed spirits, it was in this way thought to be
made secure against the intrusion of the living;
and from the horrors the natives associated with
existence there, it was spoken of with bated breath
as "the cold hell."

To propitiate the gods and place themselves
right with the powers of the spirit world, was,
however, the policy of the Romans. A singular
proof of this is met with a few miles from Carlisle, where an altar has been discovered and is to
be seen, dedicated to a deity absolutely unknown
in Rome but worshipped in Britain.

Of the colonia and municipium at Inveresk,
little, if any, information can be obtained from
the earliest accounts of the Romans in Britain.
The topographical details given in these are
fragmentary, often inaccurate and altogether insufficient to be of any service in this respect.

When inaccurate local geography can be met with in a highly prized production of a Historiographer Royal and in the interlocutor of a learned sheriff, no surprise need be felt nor disappointment experienced, when the historians of antiquity fail to tell all we want to know. These historians had no unrivalled Atlas or Gazeteer of Geography to which to refer, no files of newspapers to which to turn. Tacitus had to depend rather upon the tales told around the camp-fires, when infantry, cavalry, seamen and marines rehearsed their doings, and in the desire of each arm to magnify the achievements of the branch of the service to which it belonged made what it had done as big as possible. With such exaggerations to draw upon the picture became distorted and out of proportion, and localities named difficult to identfy. Enough in itself, the obstacle thus met with has been enormously added to by the ingenious fertility with which imaginary resemblances of words in form of sound have been seized upon, and endeavour made to establish claims purely chimerical.

With good reason, "Delta" says in his most valuable brochure on "The Roman Antiquities of Inveresk"—"Of the Roman Itinera, north of the Tweed, we unfortunately know nothing more,— —nor can we now expect to do—than can be gathered through the geographical haziness of

Ptolemy, who is far less distinct in his northern than in his southern charts; from his emendator, Richard, the monk who flourished in the fourteenth century; or from the still more unsatisfactory Ravenna Tables which are often inextricably confused and contradictory. With these three, and a few scattered passages of Bede and Gildas before them as their guides, our more modern writers on the Roman remains of Scotland have been left to the free scope of their fancies, in the application of recorded ancient names to particular places. Indeed, not above four or five sites among us can be distinctly affirmed to have been permanent military stations with adjacent Castra Æstrita, and with dependent colonia and municipia, as demonstrated by fosse and rampart lined with stone,—by the ruins of dwelling-houses and of sacella for family worship,—by the remains of harbours and aqueducts, causeways, and public baths. All these we know to have been found at Inveresk, yet, with all these, Inveresk was, until of late, almost totally overlooked and unmentioned."

Scarcely less emphatic in reprobation of what he calls phonetic etymology is the scholarly Skene. Even he, however, has not been proof against it, for in quoting from Bede mention of a town named Giudi, he builds upon an "if" a probable derivation of Inchkeith, and establishes the locality of the said town. Now, "if," is not accepted in any of the six books of Euclid as an equivalent for "which is demonstrated," nor can it be held to be so here, especially since, in the splendid work where this *if* has slipped in, the Esk is spoken of as in Haddingtonshire.

To some, this question of groping in the grey-past, blindman's-buff fashion, after identification of places named in ancient writings may seem hardly within the scope of a work like the present. We are quite aware it may be found fault with as occupying space that might have been better employed. But it may have more to do with our subject than at first sight appears, and believing it has, we allow it to stand; not forgetting that Lord Hailes tells of having somewhere read of a Frenchman who charged Cæsar with being pedantic, because he wrote his commentaries in Latin. This is no new-fangled subject. Exactly two hundred years ago Thomas Innes took his degree as M.A. at Paris University, and some years afterwards he spent a winter chiefly in the Advocates' Library, Edinburgh, collecting materials for his able Essay on the Ancient Inhabitants of Scotland. With singular felicity and penetration he deals with his subject, and ascribes much of the confusion and obscurity that is still experienced in the study of our country's history through its language, to the negligence and ignorance of transcribers, and to the unfamiliarity of those of one age with the hand-writing of a previous. He points out, also, how the affinity of the Pictish, Irish-Gaelic, and British tongues, and the blending of the races when the Pictish and Scottish Kingdoms were joined in the ninth century together contributed so to revolutionize the language that, before the middle of the twelfth century the Pictish tongue completely disappeared.

History, antiquarian research and tradition agree in regard to what followed upon the Roman General establishing a station at Inveresk. Unlike the methods of merciless extirpation or woeful servitude adopted by later usurpers, Agricola is credited with having established a firm administration. He demanded obedience, and made order and justice to be respected. For races in an early stage of civilization this has proved the form of government from which most advantage is obtained. The policy of Agricola his successors continued, and its success became manifest. Buildings were erected such as the district and country had never before possessed, military works were constructed, usages were introduced which were previously unknown, and that system of jurisprudence was established to which Scotland has tenaciously clung.

Some writers affirm that the centurions and soldiers of those legions which served at the Firth of Forth took kindly to their quarters, and the statement receives confirmation from what has been discovered of the buildings they erected. We have heard the Bay of Musselburgh compared not unfavourably with the Bay of Naples; and assuming there must be some warrant for the comparison, the seeming resemblance may have been observed by the sons of the peninsula, and this northern station have reminded them of their sunny southern homes. Be this as it may, it is on record that when recalled A.D. 409 to fight for the tottering empire, they parted from their position with regret and felt it to be a wrench to leave behind many fruits of their industry, skill, and enterprise.

Chapter IV.

AFTER THE ROMANS.

UNDER the administration of the Roman governors, Britain rapidly advanced in wealth. The tribute exacted was hard to bear, but the security enjoyed enabled industry to thrive and the arts of peace to prosper. Beside fortified positions communities gathered and towns grew. The massive walls by which these towns were surrounded afforded protection against attack. In the more populous were constructed magnificent buildings, worthy of Rome herself in respect of architecture. An incidental notice by Bellesheim of a fountain at Carlisle, "the wondrous work of Roman hands," indicates how greatly the resources of Britain had been developed and to what noble purposes they were in part applied.

Nor was the influence of western civilization confined to towns. The provincial Briton of position imitated his military masters and conformed to their mode of living. There thus arose villas provided with all the comforts common to an Italian noble's home. In many a secluded spot were then first seen the counterparts of the mansions and country houses of more modern times. In these villas luxury abounded, golden vessels were used, jewelled armour was worn, banquets were spread, and revels held. These old times have been thought to be rude and barbarous, but in them were a rough refinement and a heroic chivalry, undaunted courage in the face of danger coupled with lamentable weakness in presence of temptation—the human nature of the nineteenth century reflected in that of the fifth and sixth.

But when the Roman legions had departed, and the firm hand that could shield as well as compel was no longer felt, a time of unrest and trouble set in. Across the sea tidings of the fertility of the land reached the fair-haired Frisian farmer folk, and they were not slow to come to fight and settle. Pinched circumstances at home, prospect of plenty abroad have ever set up the problems which emigration and immigration seek to solve. Among the first to descry the keels of the Teutons making headway for the shore were the men of Lothian. An estuary or navigable river offered the readiest access from the great sea, bend or bay provided shelter, and a gravelly bed afforded the anchorage and safe landing indispensable if a footing was to be maintained among a hostile people. It is to be remembered that such conditions led to the selection of the sites of our oldest coast towns. Something more than mere conjecture, therefore, favours the presumption that the first encounter with the invaders must have taken place at the mouth of the Esk or in its neighbourhood, for no more vulnerable spot is to be met with between Duncansby Head and Dover.

That the Frisians overcame those who had been dwellers in the land for a thousand years, the "tons," "wicks," and "hams," dotted over it plainly prove. Elphinston, Dolphinston, Edmondston, Duddingston, are to the immediate south, east and west of Inveresk. Further off, Arniston, Colinton, Carrington, Gilmerton, Ormiston, Garleton, Dirleton, Haddington, Borthwick and Tynninghame, tell the same tale of an Anglic invasion and the displacement of the native race. It may be observed all these *tons* are more or less inland. Farmer-folk do not want a stretch of gravelly beach but of land for tillage, and in choosing these sites, the Frisians showed they knew what their calling required and settled themselves accordingly.

Green, in his "History of the English People" and in "The Making of England," names Elphinston, Dolphinston, Duddingston, Edmondston, all near neighbours of Inveresk, as reminders of the Elphins, Dolphins, Doddings and Edmonds who there first set up their homesteads; he further tells that from their blood-bond and folkmote, the Anglo-Saxon Witenagemot sprung, and that out of this germ the whole system of public justice and representative government in Great Britain, step by step, has been developed. As confirmatory of what has been already stated, Covington, Lamington, Symington, Thankerton are little townships in Lanarkshire far away from sea or shore amid pastoral hills near the head waters of the Tweed, but directly accessible from the coast by the course of that river, and from Berwick—the fort on the bay.

Into the struggle between Briton and Teuton, an element entered which was bound to increase its bitterness. Christianity had penetrated into Britain, while the German races were still so far out of the stream of commerce, or what might now-a-days be called the tourists' track, that the missionaries of the new faith had never reached them. Unchristianised and dwellers in the heath, heathen came to be synonomous with non-Christian. Of this struggle we can best learn from Aneurin the bard and Gildas the historian, who were probably eye-witnesses, certainly contemporaries of the events they record in song and story. Gruesome is the narrative of Gildas. War in its most appalling wantonness he portrays. The very confusion of his tale points to its having been written amid the terrible commotion. A battle lost meant a town destroyed, promiscuous slaughter, and the unburied dead left to feed the eagles or beasts of prey.

Aneurin in the "Gododin" sings a rhythmic weird battle dirge, for the flower of British chiefs

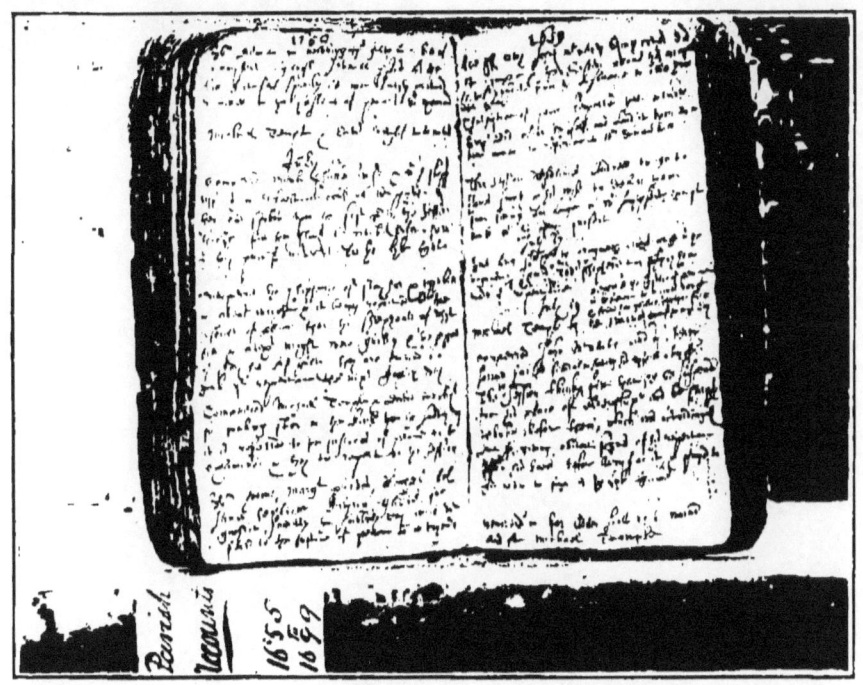

FACSIMILE OLDEST SESSION MINUTE-BOOK.

slain in the decisive and disastrous encounter at Catraeth and Gododin. The battle lasted throughout an entire week, and the Britains were completely vanquished. The scene of this conflict is placed by different interpreters of the poem in districts so far apart as Yorkshire, Cumberland, and Lothian. Those who favour the last acknowledge that the district extended from the Esk to the Pentland Hills and westward to the Roman Wall and the river Carron. Eidyn is sought to be identified with Edinburgh simply because of its similarity in form and sound. Sixty years since, William and Robert Chambers acknowledged it to be quite uncertain that Aneurin meant by Eidyn "the place now called Edinburgh," and no further discovery locates it with certainty. Several considerations point all the other way. The date of the battle of Gododin is variously given A.D. 570, 580, 596, and the bard who sings mournfully of it described himself as then an aged man. Edwin who founded Edwin's burgh did not begin to reign till A.D. 617. Chambers quotes Simon of Durham to show that in A.D. 854, Edinburgh must have been a considerable village. It could hardly have been the City of Eidyn two-and-a-half to three centuries earlier. But, besides the mention of Dinas Eidyn, what is to be said of the "hall" of Eidyn where the mailed warriors assembled, where the mead cup was drained; and the revelry of feasting, all too surely, left chiefs of whom Aneurin sang, unfitted for the fight. Of such a "hall" in Edinburgh in Aneurin's day, fable and legend, record and ruin are together silent.

Facts on the other hand favour the fancy that Aneurin may have meant Inveresk by Eidyn. Here were a municipium and colonia, and the remains of a Roman villa prove a banqueting hall had been also. The particulars the bard supplies being thus found in one of the districts assigned as the site of the battle, it is just as likely as not that district saw the end of the conflict, and that the effacement of its buildings followed the defeat of the native army.

During well-nigh two centuries wave after wave of Germanic invaders dashed upon the British coasts and pressed evermore for larger elbow-room. Throughout these generations, the ancient race was confronted with a foe whose policy was all or nothing. Victorious, pitiless destruction left nought to tell of who or what had been. Defeated, they only retired to try again. Made of the same stuff as those whom Napoleon contemptuously called a nation of shopkeepers, they were equally resolute and in the end successful. From them the Anglo-Saxon race has come. The lowland Scotch of Lothian is a survival of purest Early English, and after fourteen centuries it still retains a family resemblance of the parent Deutsch.

Writing of the English settlement, Green says, " In other lands, in Spain, or Gaul or Italy, though they were equally conquered by German peoples, religion, social life, administrative order still remained Roman. In Britain alone, Rome died into a vague tradition of the past." . . . " The villas, the mosaics, the coins which we dig up in our fields are no relics of our English fathers, but of a Roman world which our fathers' sword swept utterly away." . . . " The new England was a heathen country. The religion of Woden and Thor triumphed over the religion of Christ." The battle of Gododin was won by the worshippers of Odin.

Chapter V.

RELICS OF THE ROMANS.

IN the preceding chapter it has been shewn how the structures erected by the Romans in Britain were demolished and how the memory of them came to be effaced. Just as the spade of the excavator has brought to light treasures in Babylon and Nineveh, so has it discovered the evidence of Roman greatness in Britain. Bath and Chester have been rich in revelations, and the mounds of Silchester, till very recently only supposed possibly to mark the site of a Roman station, are now known positively to have covered that of Cavella. Like these posts in the south, Inveresk passed into oblivion till relics of its occupation revived the tale.

First among these remains may be noticed an ancient, buttressed bridge of three spans which crosses the Esk close to Musselburgh Railway Station. It is now only open for foot passengers and is locally called the Roman or the Auld Brig. This designation is at once right and wrong. Wrong, in so far that nothing of Roman handiwork remains seen,—right, as to its being of Roman origin. Even though it bears a considerable resemblance to the Pont Sista at Rome, this bridge lacks certain features which pertain to those of Roman construction. But the explanation of this difficulty was at length obtained. Previous to the completion of the bridge designed by Rennie further down the stream, and while its earlier neighbour was still used for vehicular traffic, it became necessary to have the latter repaired. This was in 1809. Sir John Hope of Pinkie, Convener of the District Road Trustees, took advantage of the opportunity and had the face of one of the buttresses opened up. Inside the outer building, remains of still older masonry resting upon transverse oaken beams were found. The foundations upon which that masonry rested and the materials of which it was composed, put its Roman origin beyond question. So great an authority as Mr. Billings had no hesitation in assigning this bridge in its present form to the early part of the fourteenth century. His experienced eye, however, at once detected a peculiarity which no builder in ordinary circumstances would have indulged in. This consists of the exceptional depth between the top of the two northmost arches and the roadway above them. Mr. Billings saw in this reason to think it probable an outer casing had been put over the original but decayed structure, as has been done in providing a new head office for the Bank of

Scotland in Edinburgh. In the case of the Musselburgh bridge, it appears the Romans' work remains enclosed, but the outer walls of the old bank office were cleared away after the new shell was put around them.

The importance of this bridge was not only local but national. It formed the main approach to Edinburgh from the south for more than a thousand years, and its maintenance was made the subject of enactments by the Scottish Parliament. Mr. Kirkpatrick Sharpe says Lady Janet Hepburn "built ye Bridge of Musselburgh." After the loss of her husband, Lord Seton, who fell at Flodden, Lady Janet, in her widowhood, applied much of her wealth in benefactions. She was the first prioress of the nunnery at Sciennes near Edinburgh, and a liberal contributor to its erection. Had Lady Janet done what Mr. K. Sharpe attributes to her, the bridge would not have needed mending so soon as 1597, as we learn from an Act of the Scottish Parliament it did. This looks more like an "old shoe" requiring to be "reclouted."

The discovery of remains already mentioned and the acknowledged existence of Roman roads to and from this bridge, entitle it to a foremost place among existing Roman relics at Inveresk.

A large slab of concrete within the policies of Inveresk House is the next object to claim attention. This is part of the floor of a bath found in January 1783, near where it is placed. The following from the pen of Dr. Alexander Carlyle tells how it was found and what it is:—" If there had remained any doubt concerning the situation of this Roman fort, it was fully cleared up a few years ago, when the proprietor of a villa, having occasion to take two or three feet off the surface of his parterre, there were then discovered the floors and foundations of various buildings. The owner being absent, attending his duty in parliament, the workmen were prevailed upon, by the author of this account, to clear the earth carefully away from one of them, and to leave the ruins standing for some time for the inspection of the curious. It was found to be a Roman bath of two rooms. The superstructure had been thrown down and removed, but the floor remained entire, and about six inches high of the wall of the smallest room, which was nine feet long and four-and-a-half wide. There was a communication for water by an earthen pipe through the partition wall. The other room was fifteen feet by nine. The floors of these, and of the other rooms, were covered with tarras uniformly laid on, about two inches thick. Below this coat there was a coarser sort of lime and gravel five inches deep, laid upon unshapely and unjointed flags. This floor stood on pillars two feet high, some of stone, some of circular bricks. The earth had been removed to come to a solid foundation on which to erect the pillars. Under the tarras of the smallest room, there was a coarser tarras, fully ten inches thick, which seemed intended to sustain or bear a more considerable fire under it than the Hypocaustum of the largest room. There appeared to have been large fires under it, as the pillars were injured by them, and there was found a quantity of charcoal in perfect preservation. The Hypocaustum of the larger room, or space under the tarrassed floor, was filled with earth, and with flues made of clay, which were laid everywhere between the rows of pillars, and were a little discoloured by smoke; a smaller degree of heat having been conveyed through them than through those under the other room. But these contrivances under the floors seem only to have been intended to preserve heat in the water, which had been conveyed heated from a kettle, built up or hung on brickwork, on one side of the largest room. This brickwork was four feet square, and much injured by strong fires. This seems to have been a kind of building used by the Romans only for temporary use. The cement or tarras, sufficiently proves by whom it was made, as the Roman composition of that kind is superior to any of later ages. It is remarkable, that the tarras of the grand sewers under the city of Rome is of the same kind; and it is related by travellers, that in the very ancient buildings in the kingdom of Bengal, the very same sort has been used. Two medals were found among the ruins, now in the possession of Robert Colt, Esq., owner of the villa. one of them of gold, much defaced, which is supposed to be of Trajan; another of copper on which the inscription is clear, *Diva Faustina.* There are traditional accounts, that in digging foundations of houses in Fisherrow, there have been found similar ruins of Hypocausta, which afford a proof that this station was not merely military, but was a Colonia Romana or Municipium; that they had many houses and buildings near the sea, as well as their *prætorium* at Inveresk; and that one of their principal harbours on this side of the Firth was at Fisherrow. From that harbour, situated where there is one at present, there was a Roman causeway, (the traces of which remained within the memory of men still living), which led to their camp at Sheriff Hall, three miles southwest and onwards to Borthwick."

Such, then, is the interesting narrative of Dr. Carlyle, and the independent accounts given by others who were interested in the subject are to a like effect. The valuable work entitled *Caledonia Romana* has its notice of the discovery accompanied by a ground plan of the baths, and a view of the tarrassed floor resting upon its pillars. The altar-looking relic in Inveresk House grounds is thus seen to be a fragment of this tarras flooring disinterred a century ago. For many years another portion of it similarly elevated upon pillars stood in the gardens of Inveresk Gate, and was supposed erroneously to have been a Druidical altar. Admiral of the Fleet Sir Alexander Milne presented it to the Antiquarian Museum about 1870.

Within this century, the vallum of the Roman citadel, which had a stone-faced rampart, could still be seen north-west from Inveresk House, but no traces of it remain.

Roman urns, medals, coins have been found repeatedly in the locality, and are mostly preserved in private collections, or have been handed over to the National Museum.

Entered by a stair from the court-yard of Inveresk House is an underground vaulted chamber. This is all now accessible of a subterranean passage over which the villa is built. The form of the arch is decidedly Roman, and the masonry indicates great antiquity. This passage is believed to have afforded means of communication between the interior of the fort and the colonia beyond. When the present approach from Newbigging to Inveresk was made last century, a part of it was come upon.

A fine collection of sculptured and otherwise curious stones are carefully preserved in Sir Alexander Milne's grounds, some of which appear to be Roman relics.

Another object to be mentioned is the mound in the church-yard, north-west from the Church. The origin of this is shrouded in obscurity. Antiquaries have wrangled over the question, some holding it to be Roman, others not. That it was used by the Duke of Somerset, and also by Oliver Cromwell as a battery mound is not questioned, but that either constructed it, may well be doubted. The author of Caledonia Romana favours the opinion that the Romans formed this mound, and after offering reasons for his preference for this view, he points out that on a point so uncertain "the one view is, at all events, as probable as the other."

Of recorded Roman remains nothing is heard till nearly a thousand years after the battle of Catraeth. In the time of Mary and Elizabeth, the first important local discovery of which we read was made. Great ado there must have been over it. Queens and statesmen thought it worthy of their consideration. Queen Mary dispatched a special messenger to the bailies of Musselburgh with her royal commands. The ambassador from the Court of St. James' made it the subject of official letters. Flattered and fluttered their honours the bailies doubtless were by the arrival of a page in ruffles and lace, and when the queen's letter was delivered to them with courtly obeisance by its youthful bearer. How proud some of Musselburgh's modern civic magnates would have been to have had such an experience? With reference to this business Queen Mary's Treasurer's book has the entry following :—" April. 1565. Item, to ane boy passand of Edinburgh, with ane charge of the queen's grace, direct to the baillies of Musselburgh, charging them to take diligent heid and attendance that the monument of grit antiquitie, now fundin, be nocht demolishit nor broken down xii. D."

Mr. Randolph, English ambassador, wrote letters to the Earl of Bedford and to Sir William Cecil which, preserved in the State Paper Office, are given in full in vol. ii. of the Antiquarian Society's Transactions. In the former of these letters the ambassador says, "For certayne ther is founde a cave besyde Muskelbourge, stounding upon a number of pillers made of tyle stones, curiously wroughte, signifyinge great antiquitie, and strange monuments found in the same. Thys cometh to my knowledge, besyde the common reporte, by the assurance of Alexander Clerke, whoe was ther to see y^t wch I wyll doe myself wth in these three or four days, and wryte unto your Lordship the more certayntie thereof, for I will leave nothing of yt unseen." In the second letter Mr. Randolph writes, "The cave found besyde Muskelbourge seemeth to be some monument of the Romaynes, by a stone that was found, with these words graven upon hym, Apollini Granno Q.L. Sabianus, Proc. Aug. Dyvers short pillers, sette upright upon the grounde, covered with tyle stones, large and thyacke, torning into dyvers angles, and certayne places lyke unto chynes (query, chimneys), to avoid smoke. This is all that I can gather thereof."

Sir Peter Young, tutor to James VI., also made a copy of the inscription, as follows:—

APOLLINI.
GRANNO.
Q. LUSINO.
SABINIA.
NUS.
PROC. AUG.
V. S. S. L. V. M.

"Apollini Granico, Quintus Lucius Sabinianus, Proconsul Augusti, votum susceptum solvit, lubens merito."

Twenty-eight years after the discovery of this dedicatory tablet, Napier of Merchiston interpolates "now utterlie demolished," into his account, but gives no hint as to who destroyed it. These were times of stress and storm. Only two years later the unfortunate Mary surrendered at Carberry, and thenceforth *her* royal command did not count for much.

In 1827 some interesting remains were obtained

in Sir Alexander Milne's grounds during operations connected with the formation of a sunk fence, and later, a conduit was there come upon, made of Roman tile and brick, together with a water run formed of oaken beams much decayed.

An entire volume might be occupied, were it attempted to enter into a detailed enumeration and description of the urns, coins, Samian ware, etc., etc., that have been found at different times in the parish, but this space forbids. Among the later finds may be mentioned a Denarius of Trajan got in the manse garden about 1864, and a particularly fine Roman urn, come upon when the foundations of Delta House, Inveresk, were excavated. The former was sent by Rev. Mr. Beveridge, the latter by Mr. John Gavine, to the Antiquarian Museum.

Some notice must now be taken of the Roman roads which traversed the parish. In Patten's "Expedecion of his Grace of Somerset;" that chronicler of the campaign furnishes a very detailed description of the locality at the time of the battle of Pinkie, in which this passage occurs :—" Fro this hil of Fanxside Bray descended my Lorde's Grace, my Lord-Lieutenant and another, along before their câpe, (camp,) within less than ii flights shottes, into a lane or strete of a xxx feet brode, fenced on either side with a wall of turf, an elle of height; which way did lead straight northwards, and nie to a church called Saint Mighaels, of Undreske." Here, then, was one of the Roman roads leading to the fort, as this description exactly tallies with what is yet to be found of Watling Street elsewhere. On till the beginning of last century, the remains of the Roman harbour at Fisherrow, and of the *via* which led to and from it continued to exist. Adam de Cardonell the antiquary, and Maitland the historian so state. One branch of this *via* led south-west by way of Dalkeith, another proceeding to the west, crossed Brunstane Burn, passed south of where Portobello has been built, onwards east of Restalrig Church and village, across the Water of Leith at the foot of Weigh House Wynd and thence to the Roman Wall.

In 1742, a seaman who served under Admiral Vernon in the Spanish Main, and was present at the battle of Porto Bello, built a cottage in sight of the sea on a lonely spot near the road just described between Musselburgh and Edinburgh. That cottage he named after the engagement. It remained standing till 1851, the old thatched house of Portobello. A relative of the present writer, who died in 1850, remembered it, solitary and alone. From this beginning, the popular watering-place which bears its name has grown. Ambitious to become a port like the two older towns on either side, a thousand loads of stones were carted about 1780 from the Roman road close by, to the mouth of Duddingston burn, to form a harbour. A further portion of the causeway was used in building the wall alongside the public road which encloses Craigentinny farm, and which can be seen to consist almost entirely of cobble stones for a considerable distance.

Chalmers, who collected materials for his Caledonia with the utmost diligence says, "It is certain, as remains attest, that a Roman road led from Inveresk to Cramond, along the coast of the Forth." Than these roads and these remains, no better proof is needed to show Inveresk to have been a Roman Station, which Emperors and their lieutenants highly valued. We admit that this may not agree with the conclusions which others have arrived at, and that the pages of many writers on the subject may be perused in vain for any reference at all to Inveresk as a Roman Station. But this by no means sets that claim aside or proves it to be unfounded. The secret which every ray of light reveals, the wisest and most learned failed to observe till far on in the present century, but the germ to which science owes the splendid results of spectrum analysis was none the less present in every sunbeam. Because two of the most eminent of Scottish analytical chemists failed to detect a fatal impurity in water

PINKIE HOUSE.

taken from a proposed source of supply for Musselburgh, and a third by a happy inspiration applied the required test and proved the presence of esparto liquor, the latter, simply because he stood alone was not to be discredited. On the contrary it was he who saved the community from the carrying forward of a scheme which would have proved a serious blunder, but which would certainly have been proceeded with, amid popular approval, had his report been in like terms to the other two.

"From all the circumstances, Inveresk Hill appears to have been a great station" is the testimony found in Gough's Camden. That the prætorium stood where St. Michael's fane was reared appears certain. Sir Robert Sibbald writes:—"Et non longe a Musselbrugo versus meridiem sita, villa de Inveresk, que fluvio Esk, ad quem sita est, nomen habet; ubi Castri Romani vestigia ceruntus, ubi nunc Templi cœmiterium jacet."

Chapter VI.

ST. MICHAEL'S OF INVERESK.

CHRISTIANITY obtained a footing in Britain and made many converts during the Roman period. To Palladius, the Orygynale Cronykil of Andro of Winton, ascribes the honour of being the pioneer missionary of the new faith. Be that as it may, the battle of Gododin, in the sixth century, was between professed Christians and worshippers of Wodin. If we accept the legend of St. Monenna of Ireland, the church of Saint Michael the Archangel at Inveresk was founded, erected and dedicated before that disastrous battle. As it appears in Celtic Scotland the legend tells that the early Scots of the sister isle came to Alban, not only to conquer but to convert. Saint Monenna is said to have founded seven churches in Scotland, and these at the principal fortified positions. Inveresk has been shown to be one of the latter, and so to rank among the number of mystic meaning. To place her title beyond question, one version of the legend is thus explicit:—"Apud Edinburgh in montis cacumine in honore Sancti Michaelis alteram edificavit ecclessiam;" which can be read, "Near

ST. MICHAEL'S OF INVERESK.

Edinburgh a second church was reared in honour of Saint Michael, on the summit of the mount." No description could better point to Saint Michael's of Inveresk, Saint Michael's of Linlithgow being attributed to the same founder in the legend. To no church in Edinburgh can it apply. The seven churches said to have been erected by Saint Monenna are represented to have been planted at important places. This corresponds with apostolic practice. It was to seats of population that the first ambassadors of the Cross betook themselves, and through the converts thus made, the gospel spread into regions more sparsely peopled. The two churches just named, dedicated to St. Michael, are upon eminences. This, again, agrees with the practice of the early church, as Michael was by it regarded, pre-eminently, the guardian of mounts.

Saint Monenna died in 519, Saint Giles in 541, Saint Cuthbert in 687. Edwin, who founded Edinburgh, did not begin to reign till 618. Saint Michael's, Inveresk, must have been in existence before any of these dates. But it may be objected why should Edinburgh be mentioned in connection with an event which took place before it was in existence? This is not difficult to account for. Monenna's zeal only received recognition by the Church, long after her life of pious endeavour. Centuries pass before canonization is conferred, and not till then does the legend of the saint take definite form. Before the legend passed as current coin, Edinburgh had arisen, and what St. Monenna had done *near it*, found its proper place in the story. Proverbs have been well styled the crystallized wisdom of the past, and so legendary tradition tells frequently a more truthful tale than written page which owes its origin to a partisan pen.

Dedications to St. Michael were numerous throughout Christendom. In the time of St. Monenna, Art had not yet been employed as the handmaid of Religion. But men's minds were moved and their lives influenced by the thoughts which Art afterwards gave expression to by sculpture, on the canvas, or in painted window. The symbolism met with in representations of St Michael help to explain the secret of the veneration he received. The particular idea associated with the patron saint of Inveresk may be held to be that which the crest borne upon the old common seal of the burgh of Musselburgh embodies. By it Saint Michael is represented as a mailed warrior with outspread wings, youthful, vigilant, valiant, the spear in his right hand, the cross upon his shield, and the vanquished dragon prostrate beneath him. In this is signified one of the oldest and most precious hopes that ever cheered man's heart, the ultimate triumph of the spirit

ST. MICHAEL'S OF INVERESK.   53

of good over the spirit of evil. As one of the
emblems of this archangel most frequently met
with, when it was a freeman's privilege to fight
and when to be uneducated in letters was accounted
honourable, such symbols had their use.

Dante says in Paradisio :—

> "To speak thus is adapted to your mind,
> Since only through the sense it apprehendeth,
> What then it worthy makes of intellect.
> On this account the Scripture condescends
> Unto your faculties, and feet and hands,
> To God, attributes, and means something else:
> And Holy Church under an aspect human
> Gabriel and Michael represents to you."

In the beginning of the sixth century, when
St. Michael's of Inveresk was founded, churches
in Britain had no such aids, but the thoughts
suggested by the emblem just described are old
as Egyptian hieroglyphics, and are to be found
among them. Most probably the first church
erected at Inveresk would be of wattle and mud,
thatched, possibly with heather.. Bede informs
his readers that the church of St. Peter's at
York, then the most important of British cities,
was built of wood in the seventh century. Stone
was not generally used in church building before
the tenth or eleventh. The Church of St. Michael's
at Inveresk may have been erected earlier. When
first mentioned, in the time of Malcolm Canmore,

the district attached is called Musselburghshire. This is indicative of its antiquity. Shire, in the sense in which "parish" is now employed, was in use for centuries before it came to be applied to an area of civil jurisdiction; or parish, paroche, parochine, had found a place in our language. So employed, it points to the period of wicker and boulder stone fabrics. That the building demolished in 1803 immediately followed the first church raised, the materials of which it consisted, and the design, appear to suggest. Ample concurrent testimony establishes the fact that it was mainly constructed of the materials of the Roman fort which lay conveniently at hand, while its central and earliest part was of a style clearly antecedent to Romanesque. Parallelogram in form, without apsidal annex, its windows small and square, to Norman or Gothic it was not beholden. Like its successor, or St. Clements at Rome, one of the most interesting of all the churches in Christendom, of outward beauty it had little to boast.

Sheriffdoms, in the present meaning of that term were formed in 1305 and Ive de Addeburgh was the first appointed to that of Edinburgh, Haddington and Linlithgow. Malcolm Canmore, by whose charter to Dunfermline "the whole shire of Musselburgi" is conveyed, began to reign in 1056, two centuries and-a-half before. It can thus

ST. MICHAEL'S OF INVERESK.

be demonstrated that "shire" in the latter connection must have had a different significance than in the former, and that it does not imply a separate seat of a "shirra's" oversight.

By legend, it is seen how early Inveresk became possessed of a Christian church. History follows close upon legend's heels. Bede tells that the gospel was preached in East Lothian in the sixth century, and as the "wattyr" of Esk formed the boundary of Northumbria, from west and east the glad tidings were brought to it. In the seventh century Simeon of Durham gives it this notice: " Et tota terra quæ pertinet ad monasterium Sancti Baltheri quoad vocatur Tyningham, a Lambermore, usque ad Escemuthe." Mention is again made of Inveresk when that part of Northumbria which extended from the Tweed to the Firth of Forth became a permanent part of Scotland. When this cession was made in 1020 the fortunes of the " Esclesia de Muskilburg" became linked to those of St. Andrews instead of to Lindisfarne, and the parishioners of Inveresk were thus among the first English speaking subjects of a Scottish king.

In the printed Dunfermline Chartulary, the following translation of Malcolm Canmore's charter annexing Inveresk to Dunfermline appears:—

" Autograph—

In the name of the Holy Trinity, I, Malcolm

by the Grace of God, King of Scots, of my royal authority and power, with the confirmation and testimony of Queen Margaret my wife, and of the bishops, earls, and barons of my kingdom, the clergy also and the people acquiesing.

Let all present and future know, that I have founded an abbey on the hill of the infirm in honour of God Almighty, and of the Holy and undivided Trinity, for the safety of my own soul and of all my ancestors and for the safety of the soul of Queen Margaret my wife, and of all my successors: for I have granted, and by this my Charter confirmed to the foresaid abbey all the lands and towns of Pardasin, Pitnaurcha, Pittecorthin, Pethachichin, Lawar, Bolgin, and the shire of Kirkaludnt and Inneresc the lesser, with the whole shire of Fofriffe and Musselburge, with all their pertinents, as well in chapels and tithes and other oblations, as in all other things justly belonging to these lands, towns, and shires, as freely as any king ever granted or conveyed any gifts from the beginning of the world to this day. Witnesses, Ivus, Abbot of the Kelledees, Mackduffe, Earl, Duncan, Earl, Arnald, Earl, Neis son of William, Merleswam. At Edinburgh.

Agreeing with the Autograph in all respects.

(as added by) S^r Ja. Balfour, Lyone."

At the time when by this Charter Inveresk became subject to Dunfermline, a new era began and a new element was introduced into Scottish society. Ecclesiastical buildings became more numerous, substantial and stately. The ravages of William the Conqueror in England forced many of the wealthy to seek a refuge in Scotland where they were welcomed by Malcolm and his Queen. Like the Psalmist, Malcolm, a man of war, prepared the way for a great work which David, his son, who inherited more of his mother's qualities, carried through.

The liberality of Malcolm and Margaret may be looked at from two stand-points. One view suggests that their benevolence was lavish, improvident and misapplied, the other sees in it a wise provision to promote the best interests of the people and the true welfare of the nation. To the first estimate Tytler gives a distinct denial, an emphatic no. Malcolm in his opinion did not alienate any considerable portion of crown property, the extent of which, the personal possession of the Sovereign, he holds to have been far beyond what moderns imagine. The second question, Lord Hailes, a prominent parishioner of Inveresk during Dr. Carlyle's ministry, as effectively replies to. With the native shrewdness for which his lordship was conspicuous, he thus states the case, "We ought to judge of the conduct of men according to the notions of their age, not of ours. To endow monasteries may now be considered as a prodigal superstition, but in the days of David it was esteemed an act of pious benevolence. In them the lamp of knowledge continued to burn, however dimly. In them, men of business were formed for the state: the art of writing was cultivated by the monks, they were the only proficients in mechanics, gardening and architecture. When we examine the sites of ancient monasteries we are sometimes inclined to say with the vulgar, that the clergy in former times always chose the best of the land and the most commodious habitations: but we do not advert that religious houses were frequently erected on waste grounds, afterwards improved by the art and industry of the clergy, who, alone, had art and industry. It was devotion, says John Major, that produced opulence, but the lewd daughter strangled the parent." So writes Lord Hailes of the old churchmen.

The story of the connection between Inveresk and Dunfermline can be traced in outline in a Charter of Confirmation granted by James II., at Edinburgh, 22nd March 1450, and to which the witnesses are "William, bishop of Glasgow, William, Lord Crichton, Lord Chancellor, Andrew, Abbot of Melrose our Confessor and treasurer, William, Lord Somerville, Patrick, Lord Glammis, Masters John Arons, archdeacon of Glasgow, and George of Schoriswode, rector of Culter."

ST. MICHAEL'S OF INVERESK.

In the narration with which this deed begins, King James sets forth among other reasons which prompted him to grant it that, in the abbey of Dunfermline "many of the bodies of our ancestors, kings of the Scots, lie most honourably entombed," and his solicitude that "the tranquility, peace and freedom of the said monastery may be secured and that it may not hereafter be harassed by the disturbing influence of any fluctuating affairs, but enjoy its possessions as we earnestly desire, in quiet and perpetual prosperity." The charter is too lengthy to be here given in full, but the following provisions bear upon Inveresk in its relationship to Dunfermline. The gift of Malcolm is first confirmed, then that of Hailes, conveyed by Ethelred; next those of the most excellent David the First," among the long list of which appears "the greater Inveresk, the harbour mill and fishing, and Carbarrin, (Carberry,) and the Church of Inveresk;" express exemption is given from poinding of all belonging to the monastery,—its men and cattle being particularly mentioned,—from payment of any toll throughout Scotland, which would imply freedom from burgh maills or custom; from working at bridges, castles and all other works, thus relieving those connected with the monastery from an obligation to which all others were subject and which until recent years passed by the name of Statute Labour. From King

William the Abbey received a donation of one hundred shillings annually out of the revenue of the burgh of Edinburgh, which he gave on the day of his brother King Malcolm's burial. In the accounts of the rental derived from Musselburghshire in 1561 the payment of this £5 appears. The lands of Smeaton (Smithton) near Musselburgh were the gift of Alexander II. and the great custom leviable at Musselburgh, Robert I. conveyed to the Abbey.

Papal Bulls confirmatory of what David I. had done were issued by Lucius III. in 1182 and by Gregory IX. in 1234. The latter grants right to levy toll for the repair of bridge and streets.

How important the parish must have been regarded is to be gathered from the contribution it was called upon to pay to St. Andrews in 1176 according to the ancient Taxatio. The following is the list, Ecclesia de Muskilburg 70 mercas: ditto de Cranstoun, 60: ditto de Creichton, 30: ditto de Faulau, 6: ditto de Locherwort, 40: ditto de Kerynton, 18: ditto de Kochpen, 20: ditto de Clerkington, 8: ditto de Maisterton, 4: ditto de Heriot, 30: ditto de Monte Lacedoniæ, 12.

An entry of another kind occurs in 1198. Robert de Berwick was then Abbot of Dunfermline. Simon Stury, a burgess of Musselburgh, obtained an acre of land in feu on the north side of the Esk, the payment for which was stipulated to be paid at the feast of the nativity of John the Baptist.

Three years after this charter was granted to Simon, Musselburgh witnessed a great gathering of Scottish nobility. William the Lion had a son born at Haddington, 24th August 1198, and to swear allegiance to this little boy they were summoned here. Wynton gives the following quaint description of the occasion:—

> The tothir yhere next folowand
> The mychty Lordys of Scotland
> The athe swore off thare fewte
> At Muskilbruch beside the se
> Till Alysandyr Willamy's swne,
> His fadyrs days were nocht all dwne,
> Bot his fadyr, the King Wyllame
> In all hys state and in hys name
> Efftyre that wes King regnand
> In till the kynrik off Scotland."

This William was called "the Lion" because he placed "the ruddy lion ramp'd in gold" upon his banner, an emblem that ever since has held its place upon the royal shield, and never has ceased to call forth Scottish patriotism.

Says Burns;—

> "Wild beats my heart to trace your steps,
> Whose ancestors in days of yore
> Through hostile ranks and ruin'd gaps
> Old Scotia's bloody lion bore."

In the spring of 1242, David de Bernham,

bishop of St. Andrews, one of the best prelates Scotland ever had, called together his clergy and held a diocesan synod at Musselburgh. Alpheus Bellesheim, canon of Aix la Chapelle, in his History of the Catholic Church of Scotland furnishes particulars regarding this meeting. Dr. Rankin, author of the Hand-book of the Church of Scotland also notices it. The business transacted was of the very highest moment for the well-being of the church, and the excellent spirit which guided the deliberations of those assembled may be gathered from the drift of the decrees agreed upon. Yet we look in vain in the pages of most historians for any notice whatever of this synod.

The decrees passed were twenty-six in number. The first enjoined that church-yards be properly fenced to protect them against wild animals, which at that time were numerous in the forests that covered a great part of the country. The maintenance of church buildings in repair was laid down to be a sacred duty, and the rector of each parish was called upon to provide a silver chalice and other requisites. The clergy were required to wear a distinguishing dress, not to frequent taverns unless when on a journey, not to gamble, to be pure and circumspect, and to reside in their parishes. Sacramental wine was ordered to be Red in preference to White, and directions were given as to the administration of

Communion, Extreme Unction and Marriage. Extreme Unction was ordered to be repeated when circumstances so required, and no marriage was to be celebrated except after due proclamation of banns and then only in presence of witnesses. Prayer was to be made for the Royal Family, the Church and those in authority, and sundry other provisions were made designed to promote Religion, spiritual consolation for the sick, and that Christian burial might be accorded to those overtaken by sudden death. Finally that these decrees might become a power for good, their publication in every parish church was made imperative, and, their observance was strictly enjoined.

Fancy pictures the scene St. Michael's presented when this synodical meeting took place. Its fabric yet unharmed by the tooth of Time, its area unencumbered by pews, its floor echoes the procession of priests, its roof resounds with music, its air is fragrant with incense, and its eager occupants await their work. What that Synod did, affords an insight into these old times, and shows their churchmen to have been fervent, devout, and pious. Where worship is still offered was consecrated by their service and hallowed by what they accomplished. To imagination,

"The organ sounds, and unseen choirs
   Sing the old Latin hymns of peace and love,
   And benedictions of the Holy Ghost."

So early as 669 they began to learn Sacred music in all the churches of the English, and Eddi surnamed Stephen was engaged as first singing master for the churches in Northumbria. Of these Inveresk, it is to be remembered, was one.

De Bernham may be regarded at once as a most capable administrator and a reformer before the Reformation. These decrees prove him to have had an open eye upon abuses, and an earnest purpose to further all that he deemed desirable. Scotland has never wanted instances of perverted zeal and of Scripture teaching misapplied. Before De Bernham's day there were of the clergy who had ceased to celebrate the Communion of the Lord's Supper. "We are sinners," said they, "and therefore dread to communicate unworthily." After six centuries and a-half the same faithless superstition not only lingers, but largely prevails, among the laity, especially in the north. Hence the value a right understanding as to the Saviour's dying command "This do in remembrance of me," must have had in De Bernham's time. But, that bishop has also left behind a wonderful record of diligence in duty, of which the evidence is happily furnished by his own pen. In less than ten years he consecrated no fewer than one hundred and forty-two churches. This at first appears an astounding proof of zeal in church

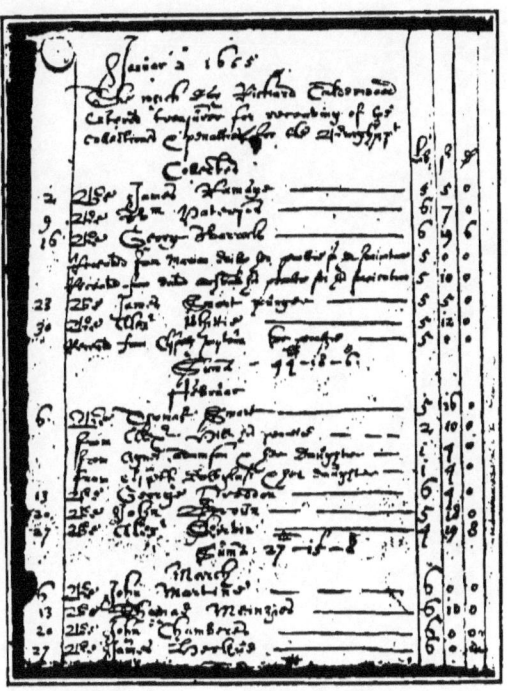

FACSIMILE HALF-PAGE OF PARISH ACCOUNT-BOOK, 1655.

building. But it is scarcely that. Rather, it is in keeping with the business disposed of at the Synod of Musselburgh, to have "all things done decently and in order," as the Apostle directs. Negligence to the rule which required church and churchyard to be consecrated, so that the one might be regarded as "The Lord's House," and the other "God's acre," had become largely prevalent, and no prelate appears to have set himself with so much assiduity to bring all within his jurisdiction to a sense of duty in this respect as he of St. Andrews. Curiously enough the pontifical offices De Bernham used when engaged in the various consecration services in which he took the prominent part has, within the last few years, been discovered in the National Library of France at Paris. On a blank leaf in it he had jotted down where and when these services were conducted, and thus is learned how busy a life he must have led. It is noteworthy that in this precious itinerary of one branch of his labours no entry of a dedication service at Inveresk appears. This, then, clearly shows St. Michael's there must have been already consecrated. St. Cuthbert's, "under the castle," Edinburgh, he dedicated on 6th March 1242, apparently after the Musselburgh meeting, and St. Giles not until 6th October of the following year. This remarkable prelate ruled over an extensive area, from the

E

Scottish border-land on the south-east to the neighbourhood of Aberdeen; and the meeting over which he presided at Musselburgh was the first provincial council held in Scotland under the authority of the Pope.

Chapter VII.

TIME OF WALLACE AND BRUCE.

IN the period of Wallace and Bruce several of the scattered threads of the parish story are found. By the untimely death of Alexander III., near Kinghorn 1286, the succession to the Scottish crown devolved upon the Maid of Norway, and the death of that princess in her eighth year plunged the country into the troubles that a disputed contest for the throne brings. Among the competitors, Robert De Pinkeny appears. He claimed to be of royal lineage, but did not press his suit. That *de Pinkeny* means *of Pinkie* seems more than probable. In the process of development to its present form it may be found in one charter as *Pontekin*, in another of 1531 between the monks of Dunfermline and those of Newbattle it is *Pinckin*, while in the Annuell of Mussilburghe-schyre, 1561, it appears *Pynkin*. It is noteworthy that all that is required to bring *Pynkeny* into harmony with the present pronounciation of *Pinkie* is the omission of its second last letter n, a strong proof of their identity. But a far more important figure than Robert de Pinkeny in the nation's annals, Sir William Wallace, once made Musselburgh his rendezvous. Resolved to punish the Earl of Dunbar for his treachery to the cause of Scottish independence, Wallace gathered to his side a couple of hundred of intrepid followers upon the Figgate Muir between Leith and the Honest Toun, 1290, and this brave band with Wallace at its head made Market Gate and Old Bridge resound with the hoofs of their horses as they pranced forward to meet Robert Lauder and Crystal Seton with their retainers at Musselburgh.

At Innerwick the patriot band encountered the traitor Earl, routed his force, and captured his stronghold, the castle of Dunbar.

About this period the pinch of famine was often felt, and many perished, while it was not uncommon for the poor to be driven to eat grass, so hard were they beset.

In 1363 Thomas Fawside, knight, is mentioned as among those who took part in a convention or parliament, which was held at Inchmartin, another instance of the important place the lairds of that ilk took in national affairs. From another of its knights, Orme, Ormiston takes its name.

As a specimen of an old Scottish manor house Pinkie deservedly holds a foremost place. Near its north-west corner is a massive tower in the style of a feudal keep. This, built by the Abbot of Dunfermline in 1390, for more than a couple of centuries was Pinkie, and up till the Reformation it was used by the Abbots as a country residence.

Few readers of Scott's "Tales of a Grandfather" will forget Binnock, the farmer-waggoner, whose ingenious strategem enabled Douglas to wrest the castle of Linlithgow from an English garrison 1311. This Binnock's successors settled in Inveresk, and became known as the Binnings of Wallyford. Lord Binning, a senator of the College of Justice, built Wallyford House towards the close of the seventeenth century. The family figure in parish and burgh records.

In the Register of Dunfermline Abbey a charter of manumission is recorded, whereby a number of slaves attached to the manor of Carberry were raised to the rank of freemen in 1313, on the condition that the Abbacy was to receive from them a two-year-old ox, or four shillings, yearly. This deed applied not only to the parents but to their children. When David I. gifted the manor, the tillers of the soil, according to the custom of the time, were conveyed with it, and became as much the property of the Abbey as anything else upon the land. Careful account of these bondsmen was kept, and only by such a deed as just mentioned could they or their posterity acquire freedom. From notices of this degraded class met with in the Dunfermline Chartulary, it appears many were the descendants of the subjugated Britons. From the frequency with which "Gille" forms a prefix to their uneuphonious names, and its significance, a servant, it is seen whence our modern "Highland ghillie" comes. Throughout the whole of the thirteenth and fourteenth centuries this condition of bondage was predominant. The names applied to farm labourers—nativi, servi, villani, homines, fugitivi, bondi, mancipii—sufficiently indicate their servile and helpless estate. The ranks of these bondsmen received a large increase in the time of William the Conqueror. Driven to despair by the sword, fire, and famine, so many fled into Scotland and gave themselves up to a life of servitude for the sake of obtaining a miserable subsistence that, for long, there were thousands of English slaves scattered among the towns and hamlets of the north.

On the afternoon of the 24th June 1314 a sad but welcome sight must have been witnessed at Musselburgh. A little band, on foam-flecked steeds, spurring on at topmost speed, rattled over the causeway of the Market Gate, hurried across the Auld Brig, and dashed along the great highway for the south. Who were these knightly warriors?

Fugitives from Bannockburn! Proud Edward and his scanty guard, hotly pursued, riding for life and liberty, the unwilling bearers of the news of Bruce's victory.

Eight years afterwards, Scotland was threatened with another visit from the English thirsting for revenge, but Bruce once more checkmated them and Edward had to return thwarted. Bruce directed all moveables to be cleared away from Lothian, and Lord Hailes relates that so well were his orders obeyed that the only plunder the English army obtained was a lame bull found at Tranent. The expedition proved a failure because supplies could not be obtained, which was exactly what The Bruce desired. On the death of Bruce in 1329, his nephew, Randolph, Earl of Moray, who had been second in command at Bannockburn, became Regent of Scotland and tutor and guardian of the young king. In the roll of the barons of Scotland 1289, Thomas Randolf, Abbe of Dunfermline is placed third on the list of Abbots, and they have precedence given them next after *Contes, i.e.*, Counts, a title long since unknown in the British peerage. The administration of Randolph must ever be regarded as a bright period in Scottish history. By it is displayed high statesmanship, unbending integrity, lofty patriotism, fearless discharge of duty, and a wise concern for the public good. Randolph despatched Roger of Fawside, a heritor of Inveresk, in 1330, as Ambassador to the Court of Edward, to negotiate a treaty of amity between the two nations, a task in which the laird of Fawside was successful. Here it may be explained that the old fortalice of Fawside Castle is outside the boundary of Inveresk, but its home farm or grange is within that line.

Two years after the treaty had been ratified Randolph was taken ill, when on a journey, about a mile eastward from Musselburgh. He had long suffered much from stone, but had borne the pain it occasioned with great fortitude. Brought back to the burgh, the best lodging the town afforded was placed at his service. It was a one storey two-roomed house with vaulted ceilings, and its site is now occupied by the dwelling at the south-east extremity of High Street, next to St. Peter's Episcopal Church. A ground plan and elevation of Randolph's lodging are given in the original Statistical Account of the parish. The house remained in the same state until the present century.

The late Sir John David Hope informed the writer that his father was most anxious to have so precious a relic preserved, but the proprietors between 1820 and 1830, proceeded to modernize and convert it into a two storey house. Subsequently it was purchased by Sir Archibald Hope, when a portion of the back wall was ascertained to be part of the original structure. During the continuance of Randolph's illness, the magistrates shewed their illustrious guest every attention in their power, and the burgesses in the discharge of their obligation to "watch and ward," did duty over his residence as a guard of honour. When the Earl of Mar, who succeeded Randolph, heard of these attentions he is said to have remarked "they are a set of honest fellows," and it is from this circumstance the Town's motto, "Honestas," was obtained. The Earl also secured to the burgh the right to collect certain customs which it enjoyed till such tolls were abolished, and roads and bridges were made chargeable upon ratepayers.

In the Register of Dunfermline we get another glimpse of the condition of society in the old burgh *circa*, 1340. Alexander de Ber, the same Abbot whom we have seen issue a charter of manumission, feus seven acres of land to a "burgens de Musselburgo," Simon Sturdy by name, and his wife Alicia, the situation of which is thus described: "Jacent inter aquam de Esk, ex occidentali porte vice se extendentem de burgo de Muscilburg, verus Nidreth." Here we see the Abbot's dealings, on the one hand with the poor slave, and on the other with the well-to-do freeman burgess. By this latter little business transaction we are reminded how much the cause of freedom, of progress and of prosperity has been nursed and promoted by the townsmen of the past, by their corporations and by their guilds. In these can be read "the nobility of labour, the long pedigree of toil."

On 24th October 1354 a charter was granted to the Burgh of Musselburgh by King David II. All the rights and privileges it had previously enjoyed as a burgh of regality holding of the Abbey of Dunfermline were by it anew ratified and confirmed.

In the depth of the winter 1355-6, the parish experienced the horrors of a state of war. Baliol had surrendered his crown and become the pensioner of Edward III.; and Scotland betrayed had to bear arms once more. David II. had been weak enough to acknowledge Edward's claims, but the proud spirit of his subjects would not brook submission. The result was Edward marched into Scotland with an army 3,000 strong, splendidly equipped. David's advisers counselled to follow Bruce's plan, and so the line of march was stripped of all that could avail the invaders. Advancing through Berwickshire into Lothian, every town and village Edward's soldiers reached were given to the flames. He made a halt of ten days at Haddington, and wantonly wrecked the Lamp of Lothian, the adjoining monastery and the town. From Haddington this mighty host proceeded by Musselburgh to Leith; and the mention of "Burnt Candlemas" in many a Scottish home long afterwards reminded of the havoc which it wrought and the misery which it caused.

Devastation from a very different agency was experienced in the district on the second Christmas Eve following Burnt Candlemas. The season had been unpropitious, the harvest was ungathered and the sodden grain still in stook. Owing to the terrible rain-fall the rivers became swollen, and lamentable destruction was the result.

To the fifteenth century the introduction of the now exceedingly popular game of golf into Scotland is attributed. Dr. Carlyle considered it probably to have been an adaption from the Dutch game of *Kolf*. It is to be remembered intercourse between Holland and Scotland came at that period to be very friendly. The herring shoals had deserted their old haunts and had found their way to the British Coasts. The maritime instincts of the Dutch, and improvements they had introduced into the process of curing, naturally sent them in pursuit of the harvest of the sea, and it became their interest to keep in the good graces of those upon the shores where they plied their calling. It is perhaps hardly so well known as it deserves to be that the prosperity of Holland owes not a little to its trade in salt herrings, at a time when cured fish were in universal request as food upon the fast days enjoined by the Church.

To the Firth of Forth Dutch luggers accordingly

came, and a brisk trade sprung up with Musselburgh. Evidence of it is still patent to everybody in the "knockhous" and clock of the Honest Toun. That clock,—and most probably the *knockhous* too,—like the essential wooden case of an old-fashioned eight-day clock,—was the gift of the Dutch States, and the thrifty Hollanders had doubtless a sense of self-interest, combined with gratitude for favours received, in making so handsome a present. The clock bears the date 1496, thus goes back for a century and a-half before the general introduction of the pendulum, and after four centuries of tear and wear continues to mark-time with commendable regularity. Its old face plates were replaced in 1883 with transparent dials, the gift of Mr. Frederick Ritchie of Messrs. James Ritchie & Son, Edinburgh. To return to the introduction of the game of golf, this national pastime was severely frowned upon in high quarters, but to little purpose. Those who imagine a people's pleasures can be controlled by Act of Parliament and changed into other currents, might find it worth while to study how powerless it proved in dealing with golf, a recreation to which leading parliamentarians now betake themselves. In the parish of Inveresk and upon the links of Musselburgh golf has been played from time immemorial, and it cannot be doubted enactments aimed at the game had its practice at this place in view. As examples of this futile legislation take the following :—In 1547 it was statute and ordained by James II. that " the fute ball and golfe be utterlie cryed doun and not to be used and that the bowe marke be maid at ilk paroch kirk, a pair of buttes and schutting be used. And that ilk man shutte sex shottes at the least, under the paine to be raised upon them that cummis not, at the least twa pennies to be given to them that cummis to the bowe markes to drink. And this to be used fra Pasche till Alhallowmes after, and be the nixt Midsommer to be ready with all their graith without failzie.

"And as tutching the fute ball and the golfe to be punished with the baronnis un-law, and gif he takis not the un-law, that it be taken be the kingis officiares; and if the parochine be inciklc, that there be three or foure bowe markis in sik places as gainis therefore, and that all men that is within fiftie and past twelve zeires sall use schutting."
"1491. Item. 'in na place of the realm there be used fute ball, golfe, or ither sik unprofitable sports, for the common gude of the realme and defense thereof.'"

Yet in spite of all this golf held its own till it came to be patronised and practised by royalty. A closing backward glance to the fifteenth century shows how some church endowments originated. The Prestons of Craigmillar were long landlords in Inveresk. Sir Simon, the laird, in 1476 burdened his lands of Cameron with an annual rent of ten merks for the maintenance of a priest to minister at one of the altars in St. Michael's Church, and in doing that he did no more than churchmen and dissenters do still when they contribute for church objects.

Chapter VIII.

DAWN OF THE REFORMATION.

IN the Parliamentary Records an entry occurs shewing that even bailies had their actions sometimes over-ruled in olden times. On 23rd March 1503-4, so reads the record 'a cause was served in Parliament against William Froge and George Hill the bailies of Musselburgh, for their misconduct in serving several writs of inquest which had issued from the Chapel (the chancery) of the Abbot of Dunfermline on a tenement in that town. The lords found that the inquest had erred in serving the writ and set aside the retour.' Such a verdict must have been appalling to their honours, and have appeared to be subversive of all municipal authority. Before Reform turned the world topsy-turvy, Bailies were Bailies and their dictum was decisive, even though it should be like his of the Canongate who maintained that a squirrel had wings, or his of Musselburgh who told an accused 'if ye hadna' a pig ye micht hae had yin, an' ye maun gist pay the fine—half-a-crown.' A worthy specimen of a Musselburgh magistrate who flourished among the twenties regarded the province of parliament to be to back the bailie. A tenement was about to be rebuilt in High Street, but an adjoining proprietor threatened to hinder the work by putting forward a claim which he could not substantiate. The point was placed before the Town Council who met on the spot and heard parties. This done, the bailie called upon the mason employed and loftily commanded him, 'Go! build that house to the skies by my orders.' 'No sae fast ye're honour,' blurted out the obstructionist, 'I'll apply tae the Sheriff for an interdic.' ' What do you say, sir ? thundered his honour, ' say another word and I'll get an act of parliament and take your house from you.'

Provost Lawrie was a more recent example of the same type. He was supremely impressed with the importance of his position. When first elected to a bailieship, in descending the Council House stair he encountered the Inspector of Police. "I'm a magistrate, sir," quoth Bailie Lawrie. Giving the official salute, Mr. Baird replied, "I am pleased to hear it sir." "Do you know sir, what would have happened sir, had I not been made a magistrate?" Poor Mr. Baird had to confess he could not divine. "Why, sir, there would have been a resignation, there would have been a demonstration, there would have been a presentation, there would have been a denunciation," and thus relieved, off the newly-fledged bailie marched stamping his

Rev. Adam Colt, M.A.

staff upon the pavement. But the Provost's self-elation sometimes had to submit to be eclipsed. A close of small dwelling-houses were required to be added to the dormitory accommodation of a private lunatic asylum of which Provost Lawrie was the medical officer. It was necessary that the Sheriff of the County should first inspect and pass them, and for this purpose he visited the premises accompanied by the Provost. Unceremoniously entering one of the houses tenanted by Beannie Moodie, a washer-woman, and who was busy among her soap-suds, the Provost announced, "this is the Sheriff, Mrs. Moodie, come to look at your house," but the good lady did not relish being caught in confusion and tartly rejoined, "I dinna care a spit, for either you or the Shirra. I s'pose, Provost, if I had come to your hoose I'd had to knock at the door an ax if it was convenient!" "You're quite right my good woman," gently put in Sheriff Gordon, "we have been very rude coming in without asking leave, we will come back some other day." "Na! na! Shirra, come in and look at the hoose, but I wus'na pleased wi' the wey the Provost cam' in," and so Beannie had the better of it with the Provost, for "didna the Shirra side wi' her."

Of much repute in the sixteenth century, the Chapel of our Lady of Loretto became famous as a place of pilgrimage. It was situated at the east end of the High Street of Musselburgh between a portion of the town's common and the mill lade. The hermit who established himself here about 1533 obtained a *petri* or piece of stoney ground for the erection of his chapel in honour of God and the Virgin Mary of Loretto. Thomas Duthie or Douchtie, we learn, to have been the name of this hermit of the order of St. Paul's. A charter of James V., 1534, confirms the feu he had obtained, and in the "Diurnal of Remarkable Occurrents" the following reference to him is made:—In this mene tyme thair come ane heremeit, callit Thomas Douchtie, in Scotland, quha haid bein lang capitane befoir the Turk, as was allegit, and brocht ane ymage of our Lady with him, and foundit the chappel of the Laureit, besyid Musselburgh." Paterson, the historian of the Regality, thinks it highly probable this Douchtie may have been a native of the burgh from the name occurring in precepts of infeftment. This chapel and its hermit attracted large numbers. Bishop Leslie gives an account of a pilgrimage made to it by James V. on foot from Stirling Castle to beseech the aid of the Virgin in his love making. The example of the king many followed, but the early reputation of the shrine became exchanged for scenes of revelry, and pilgrimages were made occasions of sinful indulgence. Lindsay gives a painful picture of departed sanctity in the references he has to what happened there. Along with part of the town the chapel was burned by Hereford in 1544, but it was speedily repaired and witnessed the last attempt at miracle working in Scotland in 1558. The principles of the Reformation had been already sown. Wishart preached in St. Michael's of Inveresk in 1546, guarded by an armed escort of the retainers of the lairds of Brunstane, Ormiston and Longniddry. Shortly thereafter he was captured at Ormiston Hall, carried to St. Andrews and suffered martyrdom.

Chapter IX.

REFORMATION PERIOD.

AT the Reformation the paroche of Inneresk and Muscilburg, that is the parish of Inveresk, was not as now included in the Presbytery of Dalkeith but formed part of the Metropolitan Presbytery. The Rev. John Burne was its minister in 1562. His stipend in 1567 was 200 merks equal to £11, 2s. 2d. sterling. A glebe was designed for him by Mr. John Spottiswood, superintendent of Lothian, consisting of "four aikers of land, whilk he possessit twa years after his entrie." His residence was doubtless the old vicarage, for the cure of St. Michael's had previously been held by vicars—and the vicarage is understood to have occupied a position very near the situation of the present manse, in evidence of which one of its adjuncts, the vicar's well, remained in Dambrae, and its water was in much request till a few years ago, when its use was forbidden and its site enclosed from sanitary considerations. References to the glebe occur in Session Records and point out its situation. These are noticed later.

After every reasonable allowance is made for the

vastly greater purchasing power of money in Mr. Burne's time, the inadequacy of the stipend he received to maintain a minister and his family in comfort is only too apparent. Nor was the case of Inveresk exceptional, all throughout Scotland the same difficulty prevailed. In this way the clergy were pinched that courtiers might profit; but as it happened in this instance it was done at the cost of undermining that mutual love between husband and wife without which domestic happiness is impossible, even in a palace. James VI. the morning after his marriage made over the church manors at Inveresk as part of the queen's dowry, but he had also handed these over to Chancellor Maitland when high in court favour. In spite of all entreaties to get the latter gift revoked, Her Majesty's marital rights were disregarded, and the Chancellor retained possession. The Earls of Lauderdale, descended from Maitland, from this came to hold the superiority of Musselburgh and the right of presentation to Inveresk. To this same chancellor Presbyterian Scotland is mainly indebted for the Act of 1592, which is still regarded as the Magna Charta of the Church of the Reformation.

It is remarkable that Mr. Burne's ministry should find no place in either of the Statistical Accounts of the parish, in the History of the Regality, nor in Gazetteer articles. This shews the inestimable value of the publication of authentic records to the cause of historical accuracy and fulness, and the great service which such societies as the Bannatyne and Maitland Clubs are capable of rendering. From the Register which furnishes particulars relative to the first Reformation minister of Inveresk, it appears that ministers' stipends were then paid at Beltym

Next in succession to Mr. John Burne was the Rev. Andrew Blackhall in 1574. From the *Register of Ministers and their stipends sen the Yeir of God 1567* he is found to have been, previous to his induction, minister of Ormistoun, Crankstoun, and Pencaitlen, with a stipend of j^c lib. *The Assignations of* ministers' stipends for the year 1576 has this entry:—"Inveresk. Maister Andro Blakhall, minister, his stipend j^c xxvj lib. xiij^s iiij^d to be payit as follows, viz.: his awin vicarage of Cranstoun newly disponit to him xxvj lib. xiij^s iiij^d and out of the third of Dunfermling j^c lib. Edward Leyns, reidare at Inveresk, his stipend xx lib. to be payit out of the third of Dunfermling be the taxmen or parochiners of Inveresk." After coming to Inveresk Mr. Blackhall had Newton and Cranston parishes also under his charge. He was a Commissioner of a province, and at the Assembly of 1580 was accused of admitting an unqualified exhorter to discharge sacred functions, but the finding is not stated. Mr.

Blackhall and his son, Andrew, had confirmation
granted to them by the king, 22 July 1582, of a
pension of xl. lib. yearly, made by the Commendator and Convent of Haliecroce beside Edinburgh, "from the twa part of the teind scheaves of
Falkirk." This pension was converted later into a
gift, and was excepted from confiscation when Parliament dealt with the temporalities of the Church,
June 1594. Such tenderness of dealing would
appear to indicate some special claim that Mr.
Blackhall had upon the convent, and that he was
one of those who formed connecting links between
"the old order and the new." Many of the early
ministers of the Reformed Church are believed to
have been priests whose accession to the ranks of
the Reformers enabled parishes to be equipped
with an educated ministry to an extent otherwise
impossible.

The year 1584 was one of much misery and confusion in Scotland. The king was determined to
supplant Presbyterian order in the Church, and
aimed at obtaining possession of absolute power.
Dismay spread through the ranks of the Presbyterians, and great activity was manifested to
accomplish the royal purpose. Cousland, Dirleton,
and Newton estates, south, east, and west of Inveresk, were confiscated for opposition to the king's
wishes, and the minister of Inveresk was summoned before the Privy Council to answer for

refusing to acknowledge the royal supremacy in spiritual as well as temporal concerns. He appears to have escaped, however, from deprivation of office, as two years later he was appointed by the Assembly one of the Commissioners for trying the offences of the ministry in Lothian. In that year also, 1586, the Lords of the Exchequer ordained Mr. David Lindsay, Commissioner of Lothian, to design "a glebe of three aikers nearest the kirk."

Mr. Blackhall was a member of the Assembly in December 1606, which agreed to constant Moderators, and named such for the different presbyteries. He died 31st January 1609 in his seventy-third year, and the stone erected to his memory may be seen in the wall of the church on west side of the spire within the ministers' burying-ground. For a considerable period towards the close of his ministry, Mr. Blackhall must have been unable fully to discharge his parochial duties unaided, nor need this be wondered at. As helper to him the Rev. Philip Hislop, A.M., a late Regent in the University of Edinburgh, was called in November 1593 and entered upon the office 1st January 1595, but died in the following year. Mr. Adam Colt, who succeeded, was admitted to the charge nine years before Mr. Blackhall's death.

During the incumbencies of Mr. Burne and Mr. Blackhall, the constitution, order, and government of the Church were in the main settled. One step towards this may be noticed. Till the Reformation Inveresk was included in the Archdeanery of Lothian, called the "Archdeanery of St. Andrews besouth Forth," but in 1581 a group of adjacent parishes including it was formed into the Presbytery of Edinburgh—the first of its kind in the kingdom. Others in due course followed, and those constituted in 1586 received royal recognition. The work of organisation went on; presbyteries were acknowledged as Courts of the Church; and the whole of Scotland was mapped out in this manner. In giving effect to this localization scheme the General Assembly, in July 1591, disjoined Inveresk from the Presbytery of Edinburgh and attached it to that of Dalkeith, in which it was enrolled 28 October following. So one of Scotland's most ancient parishes was deprived of its rightful place in her oldest Presbytery.

Chapter X.

MINISTRY OF MR. ADAM COLT.

THE third holder of the incumbency after the Reformation was a man of mark, and an able, diligent, and dignified minister. Mr. Adam Colt was appointed to the charge at the time when the Chancellor of Scotland, Alexander Seton, Lord Dunfermline, had one of his residences at Pinkie, and more than any other of the ministers of the parish he was brought into close contact and frequent conflict with the reigning sovereign in times of difficulty and danger. If, as a recent historian says of James VI., "an immortality of mischief seems to have been conferred on this foolish king," and if he were "the wisest fool in Christendom," as another has it, the position of Mr. Colt was one which required the exercise of much discretion and rare firmness.

Mr. Adam Colt was born in Perth in 1562, and was the son of a worthy elder and respected magistrate of the Fair City. His family was of good position, possessed considerable social and Court influence, and as his descendants have been connected with the parish onwards to the present generation, something of his family history may here be introduced.

During the fourteenth, fifteenth, and sixteenth centuries many of the name of Colt appear to have resided in Perthshire and the neighbouring counties, but it is claimed that a settlement had been effected in Scotland by the family at a much earlier period, and that they are descended from Colpach (*i.e.* Gaelic for "the Colt,") chief of a powerful clan as far back as the ninth century. Whether the place-name Corpach, at the southern extremity of the Caledonian Canal, is a corruption of Colpach we have been unable to ascertain, but it seems by no means improbable. Many other place-names in abundance show how widespread and influential members of the family must have been in early times; and charters and other records only add confirmation. For example, John de Colt had a charter, *apud Sconem* 12 Feb. 1228. Colt, or Cults in Aberdeenshire was originally held by John de Colt, and remained in his family till 1390, when it was conveyed by Catherine Colt to her husband, Sir John Forbes. Coltbridge, on the west of Edinburgh, in the reign of David II. belonged to 'Iohes, otherwise John de Colt, who married Beatrice de Lestalrik (Beatrice of Restalrig); and East and West Coates are unquestionably other local renderings of the family name.

The father of the Rev. Adam Colt of Inveresk was Blaise Colt, who inherited among other heritages the property of Leonardley, Perth, and which now, as near as may be, forms the present parish of St. Leonard's. Mr. Blaise Colt's signature as a magistrate appears, along with that of King James, who was at one time provost of the city, in the Perth burgh records. Mr. Adam Colt's mother was Geils (Egidia) Fleming, and through her he became related to Lord Chancellor Maitland, a relationship which gave him a powerful friend in high places.

Adam, destined to become minister of Inveresk and ancestor of the Colts of Inveresk and Gartsherrie, was the seventh and youngest son of this worthy couple. He received his education at Perth and St. Andrews. He entered St. Salvator's College in his eighteenth year, and became M.A. three years afterwards. When only twenty-four he was elected one of the Regents of Edinburgh University, then called King James the Sixth's College, and among his students he had the future Sir Thomas Hope of Craighall, afterwards a liberal contributor to the building and funds of the college. In Crawford's history of the college, the following account of Mr. Colt's election is given:—"In the year 1586, five years after the original foundation of the University (the fear of the plague being removed,) the Maisters and Students of the College returned and prosecuted their courses. In the beginning of October, Mr. Charles Lumisden demitting, and it being thought fit that ane third class should begin, Programmes were set forth to invite able spirits to give tryal for two Regent's places. After public dispute for tenne days be six young men, ye Judges appoynted be ye Provost and Counsall declarit Mr. Adame Colt to bee best qualified for ye Profession of Philosophie (the other disputants were honourably rewarded for their paines.)

"In 1588 Mr. Adame Colte's classe being the second initiate be Mr. Duncan Narne (Nairne) continued be Mr. Charles Lumisden to the end of the second year, was graduate in August, being about the number of 30.

"On the 4th August 1591, Mr. Adame Colt, Regent of Edinburgh University, being called to the Ministry of Borthwick (whence he was transported to Inveresk, where he died of good age and much reputation for learning, wisdome, and pietie), Mr. Hislop, returning out of Germany, was the second time called to the Regency, and had charge of Mr. Adam Colt's classes."

Such is the account of Mr. Adam Colt's appointment to, and professorial work in, Edinburgh University as furnished by Crawford, but the date given in the last paragraph is an evident error. Dr. Hew Scott in *Fasti Ecclesiæ Scoticanæ* may be held to be a more reliable authority, its information regarding parishes in this Presbytery having been carefully collected from the Church Records by the late scholarly minister of Newbattle, the Rev. Dr. Robert Gordon. From this source we learn that Mr. Colt was admitted to the ministry, September 1595, presented to Borthwick parish by King James, 11th May 1596, and translated to Inveresk in 1597, the exact date not being recorded. He was already a large landed proprietor, and, about eleven years before his induction, had acquired from Chancellor Maitland all the land around St. Michael's Church, eastwards as far as the village of Inveresk extends with the exception of Inveresk Lodge and Halkerston Lodge, which are pre-Reformation buildings, and on the south, west, and north to the river bank and town's lands. But the terms on which these lands were obtained, whether by gift or purchase, cannot be ascertained. When Mr. Colt became settled in the parish, he built a residence for himself upon his own estate near the Church, and had a path formed through the grounds from the house to a doorway which can still be seen in the wall near the north entrance to the churchyard, and which even in the present century continued to be called "the Minister's walk." A small building in the Churchyard opposite where this path terminates was then "the Session House at the north stile," and nicely situated for the minister's convenience. The suitability of its site and arrangements has suggested to some that Inveresk House must have been really the old Manse of the parish, but had in some unexplained way passed from its original purpose. That this was the case we have heard argued with plausibility. Where lack of information failed, learned antiquarian fiction came in, and furnished beautifully elaborate explanation of how the transfer would be accomplished. And as an erroneous impression lingers long and sometimes is revived, it may be as well to put the matter right by showing it to be altogether wrong.

In a report dated 1627, there is stated as the last of the emoluments payable to the minister, "Ane hundreth poundis yearly of ye Towne of Musscilburgh ffor ye Vicarage." This makes it clear that Mr. Colt did not occupy or sub-let the official residence to which he was entitled, but was paid an annual sum as an equivalent, and explains how, after the incumbency had been held by Mr. Colt and by Mr. Oliver, his son and successor, succeeding ministers had a manse found them near where the old vicars had their abode. During the building of Inveresk House, to be hereafter described, Mr. Colt occupied Millholme, to which his grounds extended, and which—once the dower-house of the family—is situated at the west end of High Street, Musselburgh, behind the mill there.

Further proof that Inveresk House was not the manse of the parish is found in the Session Minutes of Mr. Oliver Colt's time. On 14th June 1659, he reported that one of the houses at the manse had been blown down upon the windy Sunday, and desired the Session either to put it up or permit him to do so, on the understanding that he would be refunded what it cost. To the latter alternative the Session agreed a fortnight later. Another Minute, dated 19th February 1671, sets forth that divers of the neighbours in the Dambrae had given in "a supplication for repairing the heid of the dyke belonging to the glebe which, through the break occasioned, horse, nolt, sheep and other beasts have entrie into the other yairds thereabout to the great prejudice and hurt of all the neighbours there. The Session agreed to have the dyke biggit with earth and stone to prevent cause of complaint and gave orders accordingly. These entries shew that the old vicarage was where the present manse is situate adjoining to Dambrae.

In the report from which we have already quoted there occurs the following in reference to the Music School, for which King James provided an endowment:—" Item, thair is ane Musicke

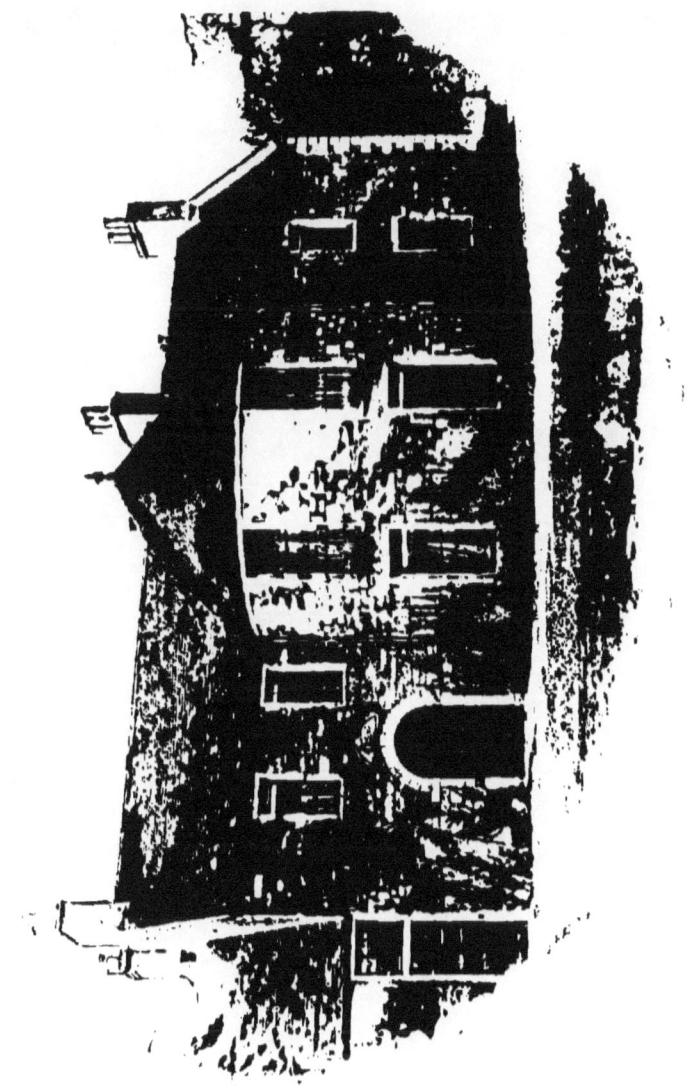

Inveresk House.

Schule in Muscilburgh quhairto umquhile King James quha lait deceissit of worthie memorie, gifftit, iij^c merkis monie furth of ye yearlie dewtie of ye erectit lordeschip of Neubottle. Thys pensionne wes gevin be ye umquhile Kingis Majestie to umquhile Mr. Andro Blakhall, minister ffor ye tyme at ye sayd Kirk ef Musscilburgh, and toe hys sone Mr. Andro Blakhall, presint minister of Aberladie, toe ye use and behove of ye said Musicke Schule, and ye sayd Mr. Andro hes sauld and disponit of ye sayd pensionne, and that the paroche and ye schule is frustratit of hys Majestie's gifft."

Such Song Schools were not uncommon at the period, and were principally intended to train their scholars for the proper rendering of sacred music. It is a pity that the Parish should have enjoyed the one it had for so short a time, and that it should have been deprived of the means of supporting it in the manner which Mr. Colt and his co-signatories describe.

The fact of two regents, or professors, in succession having been appointed after Mr. Blackhall tells of the importance attached to the charge; and Mr. Colt having been proposed as one of the ministers for Edinburgh, the year after his settlement in Inveresk, indicates the estimation in which he was held as a Presbyterian pastor.

Much it is to be regretted that the Kirk-Session

G

Records of Inveresk do not extend back beyond the ministry of Mr. Colt's son, and that no trace of any earlier minutes have yet been discovered. Contemporary history, however, is not without its use in supplementing facts which have been preserved, and in casting light upon the Parish annals. We are fortunate in having had placed at our service the valuable family information contained in the *History of the Colts of that Ilk*, compiled and printed for private circulation by Captain Colt of Gartsherrie, whose kindness in communicating particulars we desire thus specially to acknowledge.

During the year of Mr. Adam Colt's ministry at Borthwick, Scott's *Fasti* states that he "was one of those appointed by the General Assembly for a conference with the Commissioners of his Majesty." Now this must have been an important duty to entrust to a minister newly entered upon his first charge. But, important as it undoubtedly was, Mr. Adam Colt had already had considerable experience in trying circumstances, and had been resident in the metropolis at a time of great excitement and revolution. The turbulence of rival factions had brought the country more than once to the vĕrge of anarchy, and the armed bands which powerful nobles controlled had not been slow to plunge large districts into all the horrors of a state of war. Civil discord had been fomented with English intrigue for the undisguised purpose of weakening the country, and the accredited agent of Elizabeth blushed not to avow he hoped that peace and the linking of all the Scottish nobility would never be. To these hindrances to stable government the friends of the Reformation and the adherents of the old faith added their mutual abhorrence, and rendered the position of the young king one of peril and perplexity.

In his childhood and youth the Estates of the Realm entrusted the training of the heir to the throne to competent men. Chief of these was George Buchanan, one of the greatest of Scotland's scholars, a strict disciplinarian, of whom and the tawse James retained unpleasant recollections; but of the learning he acquired, and the skill in argument to which he attained he was inordinately proud. From being the victim of treachery and treason, and the object of unbridled clerical invective, he braced himself in early manhood to assert his position, and to bring his unruly subjects into subjection to law. Nor yet did he venture to claim—

"The right divine of kings to govern wrong."

In the spring of 1596 affairs were in this state, and James returned to Holyrood from the enjoyment of hunting, of which he was passionately fond, for the express purpose of attending the meeting of Assembly and delivering an oration.

On the 25th of March the king appeared in the Assembly, accompanied by an escort of the highest nobles, and was warmly welcomed by the Moderator in the name of his brethren. In his speech James bore himself right royally, and discoursed upon the affairs of Church and State with wisdom and discretion. He declared his zeal for religion, and that he esteemed it greater honour to be a Christian than to be a king. One ambition only fired him, and it was to make himself a reputation "as the establisher of religion, and the provider of livings for the ministry throughout his whole dominions." Pleading for paid troops and a standing army, he said, "The times were changed since their forefathers followed each his lord or his laird to Pinkie Field; a confused multitude, incapable of discipline, and an easy prey to regular soldiers, as the event of that miserable day could testify. . . . Since then the fashion and art of war had entirely altered; and he protested it was a shame that Scotland should be lying in careless security, whilst all other countries were up and in arms."

The favourable effect produced by this procedure was increased by the action which immediately followed. By a royal message the king caused intimation to be given to the Assembly that it was his resolution to have ministers appointed to all the kirks in Scotland, and arrangements made to provide them with sufficient stipends as far as could be done. And to accomplish this he asked the Assembly to appoint commissioners to meet in conference with the councillors he had appointed, and to fix upon a plan to give his resolution effect. This, then, was the duty to which Mr. Adam Colt was called, and in discharging it there can be little doubt he would be brought into close contact with Lord Dunfermline, then chief of the Octavians, and busy "bigging for himself a braw house at Pinkie." What influence that may have had in procuring Mr. Colt's transference to Inveresk it is impossible at this distance of time to learn; but it is not likely to have been without effect, and to have had something to do with that friendship and respect which King James so long and firmly cherished for the frank and fearless minister of St. Michael's.

The amicable relations between the Crown and the Kirk just noticed were of but short duration. Each side was eager to take advantage of the other, and the boundary line which separates lawful civil jurisdiction from undefined spiritual independence a never-failing source of trouble. Toleration was a virtue little recognised, and Christian charity a duty as little practised. If the king in his eagernesss for greater power overstepped his obligations, there were not wanting those among the clergy who claimed a freedom in the pulpit incompatible with liberty and the golden rule which the Master enjoins. The result was another crisis in the struggle, and scenes of disorder in the metropolis that boded no good. James by this time was getting accomplished in kingcraft, and seeing an advantage gained, at once took the benefit of it. He laid the city under ban, removed his residence from it, declared it no fit place for justice to be administered, and directed the law courts to go thence where he should appoint; bound the magistrates to compear at Perth to stand their trial, and the offending ministers to be indicted. Edinburgh was aghast at this, and sued for the royal clemency. James, meanwhile, prolonged the anxiety, but ordered a meeting of the Estates and of the General Assembly to be held at Perth on the 1st of March following. Of this Assembly Mr. Adam Colt was a member. The king had secured the attendance of a "sufficient number" of subservient members, and boldly sought to overturn Presbytery and to replace it with Episcopacy. In person he submitted a series of craftily-framed Articles, upon which he called the Assembly to pronounce, expecting to entrap them into taking up an untenable position. According to Spottiswood all that James desired was to see "a decent order established in the Kirk, which should be consistent with the word of God, the custom of primitive times, and the laws of the realm." So easy is it to claim Scriptural authority upon occasion to suit a purpose. The gage of war was thus thrown down, and not till the long, sore struggle was ended, had the land or the Kirk rest. In looking back upon the part which Mr. Adam Colt took in that trying time, it is difficult to decide whether most to admire his bearing as a Christian minister or the gentlemanliness of his conduct, ever in harmony with Paul's needful but much-neglected counsel, "be courteous." To please the king he never cringed, to defend the right he ever dared, and the dictates of his conscience he unflinchingly obeyed. Such a character and such an example was not without effect, and James himself was not proof against it. Differ from each other they undoubtedly did, and unpleasantness sometimes arose in consequence, but the king could not fail to recognise the honesty of the minister's heart, and the sincerity of his convictions. Intercourse with Mr. Colt his Majesty therefore courted, and counsel from him he sometimes sought. It is not, therefore, surprising to find that he both visited and corresponded with him, and that the chair which the king used upon his visits at Inveresk House is still carefully preserved among family relics at Gartsherrie. An important letter to him from the king we will give in as close a rendering of the original as possible; and here we note the following entry, relative to it, taken from the Lord Treasurer's accounts preserved in H.M. Register

House, Edinburgh :—"Item, to ane boy passand of Edinburgh (to Inveresk House) with clos ltres (letters) that come from his Matie (Majesty) to Mr Adame Colt xiij^s iiij^d, May 1606."

Mr. Adam Colt was a member of the Assembly held at Edinburgh, May 1601. At that Assembly he was appointed, along with Mr. James Gibson, as Commissioner to Merse and Teviotdale, "thair care and diligence pairtlie to be to appoint ministers in thair livings, and to try ye life, doctrine, and manner of conversation of ye ministrie of ye Bounds committed to thair visitation."

A notable instance of Mr. Colt's force of character and high sense of duty is furnished in this Assembly. Calderwood, in describing it, says, "When the king was headstrong to have the ministers of Edinburgh transported, Mr. Adam Colt opposed him face to face in the General Assembly on their behalf. The king's chief argument was, that he himself, who was a principal parishioner in his chief city, could not be edified by them. Mr. Adam Colt answered, that by that reason when he is angry at any minister in the country he may, if he will, have him transported, the preparative whereof had already passed at St. Andrews, which is very dangerous. Upon which the king called him a seditious knave, and asked why he supposed such a thing? "I suppose," he added, "Mr. Adam Colt would steal neate (cattle), then he should be hangitt." Mr. Colt did neither, however, and we find him again face to face with the king as a member of the Assembly "halden att Halicrudehouse," 15th November 1602; and representative of the Presbytery of Dalkeith at a meeting of the Synod of Lothian held at Tranent, 15th August 1602, where he signed the Confession of Faith, for the second time, along with Archbishops Spottiswood and Law, and others.

On the morning of Thursday 24th March 1603, Queen Elizabeth died at Richmond, and before ten o'clock that same morning, James VI. of Scotland was publicly proclaimed in London as her successor. News of this event was carried to Scotland by Sir Robert Carey, who rode post-haste, and reached the king's apartments at Holyrood on Saturday night following, after his Majesty had retired to rest. Among other arrangements for his departure, James committed the care of his second son, who became Charles I., to Chancellor Seton of Pinkie, and on Tuesday, 5th April, started to take possession of his new throne by way of Musselburgh. The three following years saw great changes. Of these, Tytler says, "No sooner did he ascend the English throne than he openly professed his adherence to the Episcopal form of government, and set himself to overturn the Scottish Church. In the short space of three years he procured the complete overthrow of the Presbyterian constitution,

and the declaration by the Scottish Parliament
that the royal prerogative extended over all
persons and causes whatsoever—civil, commercial,
and ecclesiastical." When he had so planned, his
Majesty commanded the attendance at Richmond
of Mr. Adam Colt, Mr. Andrew Melville, Mr. James
Melville, Mr. James Balfour, Mr. William Watson,
Mr. William Scott, Mr. John Carmichael, and Mr.
Robert Wallace. His letter to Mr. Colt was of
the following tenor :—

"To our Trustie and weill belovit, Mr. Adam
Colt, Minister of Godis Worde att Inveresk, att
hys house of Inveresk near Muscilburgh.

" James R.,

"Trustie and weill belovit we greit you heartilie
weill.

" Our earnest desire to entertaine that happie
peace of the Church of oure Kingdome of Scotland,
quilk with grit care and travell we left universallie
established therein att our removing hither, heviu
since ffrom tyme to tyme beene manifested be our
ltres to maist of ye Synods of that Realm and to
divers of our Commissioners be missives and instructiones, als weill verball als in writing, and
more parfaitlie ratified be letters written to our
Counsall with our aine hand purporting maist
clear testimonie of ye constancie of oure luve to
all weill affected members of that bodie, which be
proclamationes and imprentit declarationes wes

lykewise als solemnlie publishit, als ye notorietie thereof wuld be unknawn to none, but such als through senselessnesse would naither heare or see; hevin nathlesnesse so little prevalit with some incredulous, wilfull, ingrate, and malicious disposit persons, als some of them have nott forborne rashlie to centenne and disobey oure authoritie, charges and commandements, and so stubbornlie to persist in theire contumacie als theire malicious obstanacies hes forced us to intende greater rigoure agin thame thann oure inclinacioune alloweth. Yitt, farre lesse thann thair offences did deserve; and uthers have presumit in Pulpitt fullishlie to justifie ye obstinate and malicious proceedings of thair bretherin, and therewith to slaundere oure juste commandements, and lauchfull proceedins of oure Counsall; als also ye Synodis bein requirit be oure letters (and Commissioneres) directit to thame, to provide ffor thair aine pairtes, sae ffar as in thame laie, to giff us assurance that certaine actis establishit in fformer Assemblies necessarie ffor yee weale and peace of ye Kirke particularlie expressit in oure instructionis sent unto thame, maie be ordeanit be thame not to bee propound, treated or altered at ye nixt Generall Assemblie, quilk we know now toe bee flitte toe bee untuiched and owerpast att ye samen, than that aine mentione sould bee mayde of thame, leest thairbye occaisione sould arise of distractioune in ye Kirke and offence toe ourselves; Yitt thay soe littel regairtit ye airnestnisse of oure sute, als thair answeers universallie tendit toe ane prisint delaye, without anie assurance of thair performing att ye Assemblie of that quilk ffor thair ain weill wee soe airnestlie urgitt, quhairin findin a masquerade oppositioune toe oure just peticioune than we culd ever have expectit in any such case, these things and uther weichtie reesounes, have movit us heerbye to will and command you, all excuses sett asyde, not toe faile with diligence to repaire towairts us beefoire ye 15th day of September nixt, toe ye intint we maie that daie beginne with yourself and suche uthere of your bretheren als we have knawn toe bee of gude learning, judgment, and experience, and commandit likewise toe bee heere att that samen tyme, toe treete with you in matters concerning ye peace of our sayde Kirke of Scotland, and toe mak oure constant and unchangeable favoure borne toe all dutiefull members of that bodie, manifestlie knawn untoe you, quhairbye yee maie be bound inn dutie and conscience toe comforme yourselves toe our godlie meanin, and toe hear true witnessing ffor justifein ye lauchfullnesse off all oure intenciounes and actiounes, als weill concernin ye haill kirke, als ye particulaire members thairof; and that it maie bee manifest toe all ye warld that we haie embassed ourselfe for gevin satisfactioune toe all that are of that proffessioune farther than uther Princes accompt beeseenine toe thair estate. If thairfor anie turbulent spirits bee not recallit toe thair dutie but persiste maliciouslie inn undutiefull contempt of us, it maie then bee worthielie judgeit that ye severite quhilk bee thair obstinacie we maie bee forcit toe use, sall raithar bee violentlie extortit agin oure nature, ffor thair overthrowe.

"Thus hoping yee will note faile preciselie toe keep ye foresaide appoyntit daie, als ye tender oure seruice, and ye weille of ye kirke, wee bid your fareweill,

"at oure Manour of Greinwiche,
"ye 21st Maie 1606."

It is to be remembered that in the early months of the same year John Welch, son-in-law of John Knox, and five other ministers had been put upon their trial, and the most shameful means resorted to, to obtain their conviction. Their defence was brilliantly conducted by Mr., afterwards Sir, Thomas Hope of Craighall. Of this trial the celebrated Lord Hailes remarks: "We see here the prime minister, in order to obtain a sentence agreeable to the king, address the judges with promises and threats, pack the jury, and then deal with them without scruple and ceremony. It is also evident that the king's advocate disliked the proceedings as impolitic and odious, but that he had not resolution to oppose them." Little is there to surprise, then, that the other seven prominent ministers who received letters similar in purport to the one we have given were not eager to obey the king's call, but, along with Mr. Colt, held counsel together what was to be done.

They had other duties on hand, which they resolved first to discharge, having been elected as representatives from the Assembly to attend the meeting of the Scottish Parliament at Perth in July. That done, they set out for London—some by sea, others by land. Any misgivings they entertained were more than verified by the treatment they met with after their arrival at Court. Outwardly, a show of respectful recognition was manifested, but underneath this gloss was the most transparent design to compass their defeat and downfall, and to force them into becoming traitors to their country and their Church. Space forbids us entering into details of the open and surreptitious plans adopted, and of the shameful effrontery of the minions of the king in their serpent-like subtlety of attack. For months these tactics were pitilessly plied, but not one of these brave Scotsmen could be found base enough to sacrifice truth and duty, even to please a king. Andrew Melville was basely condemned to the Tower, whence he was not released till after four years' confinement; his nephew James to perpetual banishment from

Scotland; and the other six, Tytler incorrectly states, were allowed to return to Scotland, but were not permitted to settle in their own parishes.

As regards Mr. Adam Colt, an order "Givin at our Court at Quhythall (Whitehall) 10 May 1607." was sent him, signed by James, and countersigned by Marr, Dunbar, "Secretar," toe goe home and be confynit within hys awin paroche at Mussilburgh;" and we incline to the opinion that the other five were similarly dealt with. An expedient this, apparently suggested by the well-known punishment of "confinement to barracks" which defaulters in garrison are awarded, and was therefore, in the case of these faithful ministers, all the more reprehensible.

In the year 1627 King Charles I. appointed a Royal Commission to collect information regarding the several parishes of Scotland and their Endowments. Forty-nine only of all the returns then obtained have been discovered, and one of these is that relative to this parish. It bears to be "Ansueris maid be Mr. Adame Colt, Minister of the Evangell at the Kirk of Inueresk, *alias* Mussilburgh, within the Presbyterie of Dalkeith, and be John Wernour, one of the balleis of Mussilburgh, Robert Dowglas and Robert Wernour, all portionaris of Inueresk, and Thomas Hunter, in Cowsland, Inhabitantis within the said parochine, and electit and chosen be the said Minister, and sworn before the Lordis Commissionaris. To the articles set doun be thair lordschips and contenit in the charge direct to the said Minister." The report proceeds:—

"1. In the FIRST we declair that thair ar of Communicantis iij^m (3000) or thairby.

"2. The haill landis and rowmes within the said paroche ar about ane myle to the kirk, except the toun and landis of Cowsland quhilk is twa myles.

"3. Our said kirk is not united to na uther kirk, and it is ane of the paroche kirks of Dumfermling, and the Kingis Majestie is patrone thairof.

"4. I the said Mr. Adame Colt, Minister, declaires that I have of yeirlie stipend for serving the cure at the said kirk iij^c (300) merkis money and I Chalder aittis (oats) payed to me be Sir Henry Wardlaw, Chalmerlane to his Majestie out of His Hieness rentis of the Lordschip of Dumfermling, With ane part of the vicarage of the said parochine of Inueresk possest be the gentilmen and heritouris of the landis within the same ilk man for his awne part ffor the whilk they sould pay me yeirlie fourtie schillingis for ilk pleuch of land. Ane uther pairt of the said vicarage (quhilk is the tiend fifche) were possest be the umquhile Erle of Dumfermling and now be his Countess, for the quhilk hir tacksman pays hir yeirlie iij^c money, and the vicarage teindis of the croft of land callit the Holmes pertening to the burgh of Mussilburgh,

Old Communion Plate, Charter Chest, and Session Records.

and the teindis of the croft callit Hudiscroft, and of the aiker callit Thomas' aiker pertening to David Rammage and Henry Calderwood, and the teindis of the aiker callit Rude aiker, and of four croftis of land besyde Mussilburgh pertening to the Laird of Craigmillar, and the tendis of sum burrow riggis and tallies besyde Mussilburgh as possest be Jean Blakhall in Mussilburgh be pretendit richt and tollerance of the said Sir Henry Wardlaw and Mr. William Wardlaw, his sone, for yeirlie payment to thame of 1 Chalder beir, moreover I have j^c lib (£100) of the toune of Mussilburgh for the vicarage.

"5. We declair that there is ane Grammar Schoole in Musselburge, and that it is very necessary that ane schoole be there, for our said parochine is populous. But there is na foundation nor provision for ane schoole except xvij lib Scots, or thereby of annuals paid out of certain houses in Mussilburgh doitit of old to the chaplanreis callit Alareit (Loretto) and St. James besyde Mussilburgh.

Next follow particulars of the endowment given by King James VI. for a Music (Sang) School, and an explanation of how the parish and burgh became deprived of that royal benefaction already quoted.

"6. Thair is na hospital in the parish and it is necessar that thair should be ane in respect thair ar many honest decayed persons within the same and thair ar sundrie small teinds and dewties founded and doit for ane and specially thair is ane chapelle callit Magdalene Chapelle gifted to Mr. Robert Creichton for the quilk he gettis yeirlie xvj lib fra Mr. David Preston of Quhythill (Whitehill). Item thair ar four croftis land besyde Mussilburgh possest be the Laird of Craigmillar and ane aiker callit the Rude Aiker, and twa riggis We know not be what form or manner nor for what dewtie but we suspect they belang to sum alterage within our said parochine and thair are sum annuallis vpliftit be Mr. Robert Creichton furth of certaine housis in Musselburgh We know not quhat way nor be what richt and title.

"7. We knaw of na uther chaplanreis, prebendaries, nor frier landis within our said parochine.

Then follow particulars regarding the teindable lands in the parish, which may be thus summarised ;—

Property.	Holder.	Extent.
Cowsland	Lord Chancellor	40 husband lands
Lands & Maynes of Carbarrie	James Rig	12 pleuch lands
Lands & Maynes of Smeton		32 oxingaits
Inveresk	The King	13 pleuch lands
Monktounhall (1)	Feuars portioners	8 pleuch lands.
Monktoun	Alex. Hay	5 pleuch lands
Quhythill (2)	Edward Preston	3 pleuch lands
Stonyhill	Robert Dobbie	3 pleuch lands

Property.	Holder.	Extent.
Pinkie (3)	Earl of Dunfermline	15 Oxingaits
Quhyteside	Robert Fawsyde of that ilk	1 pleuch land
Crofts beysde Musselburgh	Laird of Craigmillar	Stock worth 1 chalder and
Tarress Croft	Hew Brown (Teind at 6 bolls)	Teind at 8 bolls

A perusal of this interesting report reveals how Church properties were taken possession of without scruple by private persons for personal ends with the connivance of others whose care it should have been to prevent such appropriation, and it shows how, even so near to the time of plundering, it was most difficult for influential persons on the spot to obtain accurate information or to get restitution made, from the want of any authentic records to which they could have recourse. On the other hand it shows the minister of Inveresk and the laymen associated with him to have been fearless in the discharge of duty to the delinquent and "suspect," granting no privilege and making no distinction, and actuated with a praiseworthy regard for the interests of education and the relief of the necessitous.

NOTES.—1. Teinds in the hands of Sir Thomas Outterhouse, tacksman to the king. 2. Teinds in the hands of the Earl of Dunfermline. 3. "The stok and teinds of old paid four chalders and now twenty chalders, but in respect of the multitude of laboraris," the reporter says, "we think the stok may pay yearlie *communibus annus* in tyme cuming x chalders." An oxingait or oxgang contained thirteen acres; a husband-land was two oxingaits or twenty-six acres; a pleuch land or ploughgate was eight oxingaits, or one hundred and four acres.

Chapter XI.

OLD COMMUNION CUPS.

DURING the incumbency of Mr. Adam Colt, the parish church became possessed of four handsome silver communion cups, but up till five years ago no certain knowledge was obtainable regarding them. That lack of information is now supplied.

Among the records preserved by the Session is a book of parish accounts, titled "*Liber sessionis*

ecclesia apud Inneresk,"—that is, Session Book of the Church at Inveresk. It contains, in beautiful old-fashioned hand-writing, particulars of the receipts and "debursements" for the period 1655-1669. Its first page is headed, "Januar 2, 1655, The which day Richard Calderwood entered Treasurer for receiving of Collections and penalties for the Burgh part," and its second, "The which day Robert Hislop, in Monktonhall, entered Treasurer for receiving of Collections and penalties for the Landward." An entry, Januar 19, 1655, shews the retiring Treasurers to have accounted for their intromissions "for ye year 1654" at meetings held that day, and to have handed over all money, documents, etc., in their charge. In the inventories of these, the newly-entered Treasurers acknowledge respectively as follows:—"Item, Twa Silver Comunion Cups,"— "Item, received also by ye sd. Rot. Hislop, ye two Comunion Cups of silver, ye Burgh Thesaurer having ye other two."

These are the earliest known written records of the Old Communion Cups. When, where, or by whom, made; how, or from whom, obtained, seemed points never likely to be ascertained. But the unique and splendid collection shewn in the Edinburgh International Exhibition, in which one of these cups was included, invested the subject of old Scottish Communion Plate with fresh interest, and the curiosity to learn more thus excited came to be fully gratified.

Upon all silver articles made during the seventeenth century, Acts of the Scottish Parliament required three Hall marks to be put. Each of our cups bear these, the stamp of the maker, of the place where made, and of the Assay Master. These marks, carefully examined and compared with the Records of the Edinburgh Goldsmiths' Hall, by favour of Mr. Michael Crichton, Deacon of the Incorporation, 1889, prove that all four Inveresk cups were made in 1621, at Edinburgh, by George Crawford, a silversmith, who made the Newbattle cups in 1618, and was twice Deacon of the Incorporation, 1621-3, 1633-5. The Assay Master who stamped them was James Dennistoun; his name is sometimes spelled Danielstown. He was a member of the corporation, 1613-1644.

The dimensions of the cups are, full height, $8\frac{5}{8}$ inches, diameter of base, $4\frac{5}{8}$ inches, diameter of bowl, $6\frac{7}{8}$ inches, depth of bowl, $2\frac{1}{2}$ inches. On one, in the bottom of the bowl, is engraven a shield, having three crescents within a double tressure flowered and counter-flowered, in its first and fourth quarters, and three cinquefoils on a horizontal bar in its second and third quarters. The escutcheon is surmounted by an Earl's coronet, a crescent, and the word "Semper," around the whole being the motto "*Nec cede adversis rebus nec crede secundis,"* which freely rendered reads, "Neither retreat before adversity, nor put confidence in prosperity."

This coat of arms, of which we give an illustration, is that of Alexander, first Earl of Dunfermline, who owned Pinkie House, where in one of the rooms, he had these armorial bearings placed, with horses representing Liberty as supporters, and this very motto. These still remain in excellent preservation.

In design the cups are simple, chaste, elegant, the outlines graceful and well-proportioned. The only ornament used is a band of exquisite chasing round the base. These cups are historic monuments of no common value. So long as the Church confined to the clergy the cup of blessing—as it is called by St. Paul—small chalice cups alone were used; but among the changes effected by the Reformation, all believers were admitted to partake of the Sacrament of the Supper in the manner appointed by Our Lord; and, in token of this, the Scottish Reformers directed "large silver cups" to be provided for Sacramental use.

In a letter written by the donor of these cups, "From Pinkie, 24 May 1621" to "his maist honourable good friend Sir Robert Ker, off Ancrum, in the Prence his Heighness' bed-chalmer," as given in Mr. George Seton's memoir of Chancellor Seton, a pleasant glimpse is had of this fine old gentleman. Lord Dunfermline had cultivated a frame of mind which enabled him to contemplate death without fear. He tells, Sir Robert "In bulk or banis I find yit leittll decay in me," yet reckoned it prudent not to be so ready as formerly to undertake work. However, he continued sufficiently robust to be able to use the same bow at archery that he had been accustomed to handle forty years before. In the vigour of his manhood, the Earl had been no sluggard, but had filled many important positions. From encountering "fashious" pieces of business he did not shrink. As Chancellor of Scotland, Senator of the College of Justice, President of the Court of Session, Lord Provost of Edinburgh, Chief Magistrate of Elgin, and Bailie of Dunfermline, his lordship did his duty with diligence and discretion. Little wonder as eventide approached he felt "nocht sae readie to tak meikill in haud." On the morning of Sunday, 16 June 1622, the Earl died at Pinkie after a fortnight's illness, during which he was lovingly attended by devoted relatives and his condition eagerly enquired for by anxious friends. His remains were interred at Dalgetty, in Fife, 9th July following.

Six years before Lord Dunfermline's death, the parish and burgh must have been greatly exercised over the King's coming. The recently issued ninth

volume of the Register of the Privy Council of
Scotland gives an excellent idea of the general
hubbub which that event occasioned. For the
royal progress northwards in May, preparations
were begun in the preceding January, and requisitioning upon a scale now hardly conceivable was
put in operation. Every parish had to furnish its
quota of carts properly equipped with competent
drivers, and any failure or lack of punctuality
entailed a heavy penalty. The joy of welcoming
King James VI. must have been considerably modified by these exactions. Nor were the demands
confined to providing transports for the baggage.
The royal pantry had to be plenished, and for it,
Musselburgh was stented to provide a dozen fed
oxen for the feast-making at Holyrood. When
this happened, Mr. Colt was still in the active
discharge of ministerial duty, and doubtless Lord
Dunfermline and he would both see that the
burgh, which four years earlier had received a
Charter from Queen Anne, proved equal to the
emergency.

Mr. Colt demitted his charge 3rd June 1641, and
was succeeded by his son Oliver who had taken
his M.A. degree at Edinburgh in 1621, received
license 1627, and was ordained and installed helper
1632. Mr. Oliver Colt was a member of the
Assembly of 1638, and was presented to Inveresk
by Charles I., 14th May 1641 He became his

father's colleague on 3rd, and his successor on 4th June following.

In the diary of Sir Thomas Hope the entry, "Att sevin in the morning *gude* Mr. Adame Colt, my Regent, and minister at Inveresk, deceasit, Fryday, 24th March 1643," shews the affection cherished for him by his distinguished pupil. Mr. Colt's ministry left behind a good record. He is spoken of as "hevin much reputationne ffor learning, wisdome and pietie, and ane of those accountit eminente ffor grace and giftis of faythefullness and success."

When Mr. Oliver Colt succeeded to the full charge of the incumbency the lord of the regality of Musselburgh was John, second Lord Thirlstane, whose son became the Duke of Lauderdale. This John, Lord Thirlstane, built Brunstane Manorhouse in 1639, and thus had a residence on the border of the parish, Pinkie having been expressly withheld from the grant of Church lands which his father, Chancellor Maitland, received.

For the first ten years of Mr. Oliver Colt's ministry no records remain, but it scarce admits of doubt that regular minutes would be made at the time. The manner in which those of later date have been kept warrants this being presumed.

In 1638, the sixth year of his assistantship to his father, Mr. Oliver Colt must have witnessed a memorable event upon Musselburgh Links. As

Commissioner from Charles I., who had been in pupillarity under Lord Dunfermline of Pinkie, the Marquis of Hamilton came to Scotland charged to discomfit the covenanting Presbyterians. Upon the links of Musselburgh he was confronted by thousands of that party, and all the way to Leith had to pass through their ranks.

In 1649 Charles I. perished upon the scaffold, and the following year found Oliver Cromwell in Oliver Colt's residence at Inveresk. By this time the latter had added to the paternal dwelling, and had placed his own monogram over its entrance.

Of the eventful period in the autumn of 1650, when Cromwell was at or about Musselburgh for a couple of months, many particulars can be gathered from his letters written thence, and from the incidents noted by Nicoll. Both agree that the English army reached Musselburgh on 25th July. Shipping came thither with stores, and trenches were thrown up. On the Wednesday after the arrival of Cromwell's force a reconnaisance of its position was made by Colonels Montgomerie and Strachane with 800 troops, and some skirmishing took place. Both sides claimed to have the advantage. On the 3d August "Cromwell sent in in his awn Koatche and in kairts out of Mussilburgh 60 wounded Scots taken in the late skirmish." The little knoll on Musselburgh Links opposite Linkfield House is still regarded as the spot where

Cromwell's tent was placed. About midnight of
5th August Cromwell broke up his encampment
and started on the march for Dunbar, but speedily
returned. Sunday, the 11th August, was observed
as a day of fasting and prayer.

In writing to the Lord President of the Council
of State from Musselburgh, Cromwell claims that
he was engaged on the Lord's business *rather than*
the State's, which perhaps he might reckon sufficient warrant for employing the Lord's day
morning in marching forward from Haddington
in hope of encountering the Scottish army on
Gladsmoor. Disappointed in this, the vanguard
pushed on to Musselburgh and the General followed
at their heels. He complains of the heavy rainfall
during the next few days and of the consequent
discomfort experienced by his men, but we miss in
any of the Lord General's letters acknowledgment
of the comfortable quarters *he* occupied in the
parish minister's house at Inveresk. The apartments are still pointed out which he used as living
and orderly rooms. Nor does Cromwell say more
than that he drew back to his old quarters at
Musselburgh to replenish his scant supply of provisions after vainly attempting to get the Scots out
of their strong position. Nicoll lets it be known it
was not from English shipping the fresh stores
were obtained. Cromwell, he says, went back to
the Braids " with great quantities of victual quilk

he had taken out of the mylnes, killes, and bernis of Mussilburgh and other pairts thereabout." Indiscrimate making free with other people's property, however, Cromwell sternly dealt with, and on 27th September, he had three men flogged for plundering houses in Edinburgh without permission. When at length he found it necessary to return to England twenty-eight boats belonging to Musselburgh, Prestonpans and Cokkeny were requisitioned, and proceeded to Leith to assist in the embarkation of those they would gladly see go.

Chapter XII.

SEVENTEENTH CENTURY RECORDS.

THE oldest records connected with Inveresk Church are a volume of minutes of the Session, Nov. 1651 to Aug. 1677, and a volume of Parish Accounts, 1655-1669. Remarkably full and carefully kept, these two books furnish a wonderful insight into the parish life, and testify to the activity with which church office-bearers looked after parishioners. The following are given as illustrative of the contents of these volumes :—

1651, Dec. 4.—Complained Wm. Bell, miller, upon Wm. Nicoll, that he called him a thief; the bill being proven the Session ordained him to mak his repentance the nixt Lord's day. Dec. 11.—Compeared Wm. Nicoll, miller, before the whole congregation, and made his repentance for his slander against Wm. Bell.

For the punishment and reclamation of transgressors the pillar of repentance, sackcloth, the branks, and money penalties were recognized methods of discipline, and when these failed or an offender was contumacious, the case was reported to the bailies that imprisonment might be inflicted. Of all these means being employed examples occur. Breaches of the third, fourth, seventh, eighth, and ninth commandments are most frequently in evidence, but the attention of the Session was by no means confined to dealing with business of this sort.

A Scottish comrade of an Irish artillery-man in India, used to tell how, when the black cook came one Thursday evening to enquire what was wished for breakfast next morning, Pat contemplatively scratched his head and said, "Let me see, I can't ate mate to-morrow because it is Friday;" then, to overcome the difficulty, he compromised the matter by ordering "bacon and pluck." But Inveresk folks were just about as nimble at turning a corner at a pinch. Here is how they managed to take the edge off the fast day:— "Januar. 4, 1652, Richd. Calderwood did become cautioner under the paine of 20 lib. money that there should be no extraordinar meat made ready att Robt. Smeall's banquett it being a fast day." Many such entries are met with. On January 18th is "a memorandum to intimate about the repairing of the kirk against the nixt Sabboth day." At that period the fabric of Old St. Michael's must have been sadly decayed, and notices of its requiring repair at considerable outlay frequently appear. "Januar 19.—We, Janet

Edgly and Helen Dobie (in presence of John Calderwood, baillie; John Maknaith, George Vallange and James Wicke) shall doe act ourselves under the penaltie of twentie pounds money *toties quoties* that quilk soever of us shall be found or heard scandalizing one another either privatelie or publickly, shall pay the penaltie forsaid." "Feb. 17, 1652.—The Session condescend that the Laird of Monktoun should have libertie to enlarge his seat towards the body of the church as far as the foremost pillar of the Earl of Lauddaille's seat." James Smart, David Ramage, and sundrie others also desired to have their seats enlarged towards the body of the church, and it was granted unto them. On same date, "the Session having heard the Bill of William Duncan and his pairteners and the Bill of John Maisson anent the seat before the wester loft as thir bills declared, condescend that quilk soever of them shall give most for it should have it; and lykewise the Session ordained that quilk soever of the pairties should get that seat, they should have but only one seat there, and also quilk soever should get that seat should procure libertie of the Earle of Lauderdaille and Lady Dumfermling, or they build there. William Duncan in his awin name, and in name of his pairteners, offered 50 mercas. John Maisson offered 40 lib., William Duncan immediately offered 46 lib. 13sh. 4d.

Wherupon the said John Maisson appealed to the presbytery for reasons he was to give in there." A week later, Feb. 24, another competition about a seat is met with. " My Lord Cranston Makgil produced ane Bill anent ane seat in the church. The Laird of Smeaton in presence of the Session took instruments in name of himself agt. my Lord Cranstoun Makgil that the voyd and emptie room before the wester loft is yett in contest as one of the pairties themselves declared. All pairties that had interest in that voyd rowme before the wester loft being removed, the Session was content that the business should be referred to the presbytery with the former applications." Seats at that time were evidently in request and the Session appear to have had difficulty in satisfying applicants. Bailie John Calderwood made an application with a pawky way about it when so many were craneing their necks to secure chief seats in the synagogue. The bailie " produced ane Bill before the Session to have a snuch (snug) bounds in the southmost pairt nixt to Craigmillar's yle (aisle) before the baillies seat, as would be ane seat to his wyfe qlby she might the more conveniently hear the Word of God, and he referred himself to the Session's will whatever they should injoyne him to pay for ye samine." The bailie evidently took the Session on the soft side, and he had his prayer granted, 4 lib. being all that he was called upon to pay.

Other five gentlemen obtained sittings on the same easy condition. April 25.—Memorandum to choose ane Laik (lay) Elder to goe to the Synod with the minister, and on May 2, Bailie Stevenson is chosen. May 16.—Patrick Widderspoon, is ordained to put up that seat which he pulled down, and is ordered to pay 5 merks for his misdemenour. Robert Donaldson is ordained to make his public repentance nixt Sabbath day because of his scandal agt. Wm. Moore, *tinker*, which he did. June 20.—The Session with one voice condescends that the minister, Mr Oliver Colt, should have as much room from West Craigmillar's seat towards the body of the church as would be ane seat for him and his family. Memorandum to warn the coalhewers of Whitehill to the Session. July 25.—David Bouner, Wm. Todd, David Galbraith, Wm. Stevenson, Robt. Barrowman, (presumably these coalhewers) Compeared and on Aug. 1st, made their repentance for their profanity on the fast day. Aug. 1.—The Session ordained David Sellerman to pay ten pounds for receiving strangers without advertising the minister or the baillie. Intimation made to desire all that have promised, to produce their testimonials before the Session. Aug. 8.—Robt. Simson and Agnes Ramsay acts themselves under the pain of 5 lib. and putting of them in the branks not to scandalize one another ever after. Nov. 7.—The

Gentillmen and those of the Session condescend that there should be a new pulpit. The baillies and sessioners of the burgh are content to pay half the expense of the pulpit with all that is not prejudical to them in time to come. Memorandum anent the *Disamiting* of Cousland, Disamitting written over another word obliterated.

January 2, 1653.—The which day John Macknaith was elected treasurer for the burgh and Wm. Smyth in Monktounhall for the landward. Oct. 16, 1653.—The Session condiscends that there should be a collection for Thomas Thomson in Monktoun that had his house brunt w^h fire desires intimation made there anent the nixt Sabbeth day. The Session condescends that the weekly sermon be upon the Wednesday and desires the minister to intimat the same the nixt Sabbeth day. Oct. 25.—James Brown, Robt, Strachan, and Wm. Smyth are appointed to speak to the Lawyeres anent Adam Scott's Bill w^h the minister. Oct. 30th.—Collected and given to Thos. Thomson that had his house brunt, 50 lib. Margt. Hadden made her public repentance in sackcloth before the congregation. Nov. 16.—The Session condiscends that there be a psalme sung be the presentor before the minister comes in beith the morning and att afternoon. March 1, 1654.—To tak notice of a woman that was delivered of a child in the back of the hill of Carbarrie. The minister exhorted the elders every one of them to goe through their quarters to visit the sick and poore and try anent straingers. March 5.—The minister did intimate out of the pulpit that every elder should go through their quarters upon every Sunday after sermon to try there each house and taverine and see that there be no scandal used upon the Sabbath Day. March 8.—Memorandum for excommunication of Mr Alex. Cornwll. March 12.—The minister did intimat Mr Alex. Cornwll's excommunication out of the pulpit. March 16.—It was intimat out of the pulpitt be the minister that no testimonials should be given bot at the Session table, and lykewise that straingers that had not testimonials that they should go and geit them. Memorandum, anent the aillhous in Smeiton. March 29, John Tinto declared that there was none in his house but the Laird's man and the Laird of Preston's man. John Tinto acted himself under the paine of 5 lib. that there shall none be seen druken in his house upon the Sabbath day. April 19.—Compeared, Wm. Bayne, Patrick Bull, Wm. Cuthbert and were rebuked for byding out of the kirk upon the Sabbath day. April 26.—James Brown is elected ruling elder to go to the Synod. May 14.—The dissolution of Cousland from us and to be annexed to Cranstoun was intimate out of the pulpitt by the minister according as it was ordered by the

Synod at Edinr. in May 1654. May 24.—Compeared Elspeth Gilgour and Margaret Davidson for flyting being cited, whereupon the Session requeists the baillies to put thir twa in the branks to be example to others. July 12.—The Session requests the baillies to report to them what course they should take with Jennet Bishop, Jennet Wmson, Helen Martin, who had paid no heed to the Session's summons. Apparently this application to the baillies had effect for they appeared on Oct. 3, and came under a penalty of ten pounds if they ever misbehaved again, and, in addition, all three were ordered to be put in the branks. Memorandum for a contribution to the prisoners. Sept. 24.—The quilk day fors[d] the Gentillmen and elders of the Session being frequently convened they did change the weekly sermon to be upon the Tuysday. Oct. 31—The Session requests the baillies to imprison Barbara Hintoun for her disobedience to the Session. 1655 opens with Memorandum to choose a new Session. Feb. 28—Gives Margt. Brown, who brought a testimoniall she is maryed to a Carlisle man a 15 days to bring a testificat from under the minister's hand where she did last reside. Bessie Fowler put under a penalty of ten pounds that she shall never be heard to abuse any elder or any other neighbour. To speak to the scholmrs anent their schollers for fringing the Sabbath day in tyme of sermon. April 29—the laird of Craigmillar is elected ruling elder to go to the Synod. May 29.—The laird of Carbarries receive "libertie" to make his seat more convenient, "lykwyse that he cause repair his yle (aisle) w^t furmes, (forms), that so the common people may have the more convenience to sitt upon," and he is also called upon to strike out lights (windows) "that the church may be better enlightened thby." June 19.—The which day the minister declared that the stamp mould for the communion Tikketts which was always in the custody of Andrew Calderwood was lost, as he said, att the comming in of the English army, and so desired the treasurers to take a course for a new one in respect the communion was approaching, and there was hope it might be given. The baillies in name of the burgh desyred the stamp might be helped, and seeing the old writts of the kirk did designate it by the name of the Mussilbh. kirk and not Inueresk, they had been prejudiced by the old stamp that caryed the the name of I.K. for Inueresk kirk, the which they desyred to be helped in tyme comming. Some of the landward present answered that there could be no alteration of the stamp seeing it had for threttie or fourtie years been so, and no reason it should be changed now. The business is referred to the nixt day to a more full meiting of the Session. June 26, This was anew considered, and to avoid any needless debate two representatives of the landward and two of the burghal portion were appointed to confer together and endeavour to arrive at a friendly solution of the point in dispute. On July 15 the subject was again before the Session, and in the interval the landward representatives had procured a stamp bearing the letters I.K. and O.C. standing for Inveresk kirk and Oliver Colt. The burghal elders protested against this and considerable feeling was manifested on both sides. Eventually the case was appealed to the presbytery after both parties had taken instruments. July 24. The heat shown at preceeding meeting reached a greater intensity, and a regular bicker of words took place upon baillie John Brown producing a stamp and a number of tokens bearing the letters M.C. and O.C. which he delivered to the kirk treasurer for the burgh for use at the communion. For a couple of years the difference continued and neither party shewed the slightest disposition to bring about an agreement. At length Mr Oliver Colt, desirous of a settlement, proposed to the Session to refer the point in dispute to the joint judgment of the Lairds of Smeaton, Stoneyhill and Carbarrie, as representing the landward, and Bailies Brown, M'Millan, and Calderwood as representing the burgh, to try and arrive at some arrangement that might be satisfactory to all concerned, and on 19th July 1657 as a compromise it was agreed to have tokens bearing the letters I.K. for the landward and M.K. for the burgh. Even this concession could not be accepted graciously "but with mutual provision on both sydes that the altering of the ticketts shall no ways prejudge any of the pairties in their respective rights and interests which they can claim to have to the kirk." The token of 1727 shews a further modification of this compromise and the adaptation of one token for the entire parish by the use of a monogram formed of the letters I.M.K as shewn in illustration.

The minute book appears to have been occassionally made use of for jottings to remind of business that required attention, and such isolated entries as, "anent the Communion," are met with.

May 13, 1656.—Compeared, Thomas Lowrie, John Anderson, George Thomson for drinking upon the Sabbath day in tyme of divine sermon, and they were ordained to make their publick satisfaction the nixt Sabbath day. May 20.—The Session appointed Wm. Smyth, John Hislop, Robt. Vernor, elders to wait on the collections and serve the tables for the landward, and a corresponding appointment of burghal elders for like duties on the first day of communion, with other two groups to collect and serve upon the succeeding communion Sunday. At that time the communion was held on two Sundays following each other, and in connection with each of these there were three week day services. A tent was erected in the church-yard and from its services communicants proceeded to the tables in relays. Repeated entries occur of Mr Adam Colt, the minister, having handed 100 merks to one of the treasurers, "to furnish the elements to the communion." At the communion of 1 and 8 June 1658 the collections were burghal £74, 16s., 6d., Landward, £45, 19s., 8d., together £120, 16s., 2d. Scots. Payments included such items as for expenses of taking down the tables and furmes, and aill and bread for the servers at communion, £3. Washing the communion cloths, £1. Mending "the gang brod that held to communion wyc, 12s." Dec. 9, 1556.—The minister "produced an Act of the Synod holden at Edinburgh, in relation to a second minister to be a helper to him, wherewith they were all weil content with provision they will fall upon a way for his maintenance: "whereupon they did nominate eight men; 4 in the burgh and four in the landward to meit upon Friday nixt to see if they could fall upon a way for his maintenance and report and answer to the Session." This they do not appear to have done, nor is there any minute to show Mr Oliver Colt to have got the helper he and the Synod wished appointed. July 1.—Mr George Sutie, portioner, Inveresk, is desyred to become an elder, consents, and is admitted; two days afterwards he makes application for a seat, offers £20 for the use of the pew for the privilege which the Session accepts, but about which some objection was taken, and on Aug. 12, Mr Sutie "submitted his business to the Laird of Carbarric himself." 1658, Jan. 5.—Anent the little house at the North Stile to be mended by the Treasurer. May 11.—John Masson, portioner of Inveresk, and one of the elders, of his own motion made over a seat to the Session, for which his father had paid 20 lib., on the condition that "seats and dasks be there erected for the schollars of Mussillbh. school, which the Session were very weill pleased with, and all in one voice willinglie accepted." May 26, the quilk day ane overture being made by some of the Session anent the extracting of the Acts of Session they ordained that every Act that is made should be nixt Session day read in the audience of the Session, to see whidder or no it be conforme to their ordinance, and that it be not granted or given out to any quilk somever untill it first be heard, seen, and approved. Oct. 25.—Laird of Stoneyhill elected ruling elder to the Synod at Edr. March 22, 1659. The minister communicated a letter which came in relation to a contribution to help to big a bridge upon Tyne water. The Session all and everie one of them that were present refused to consent or to give any contribution to that object, in respect they were not able, but were greatly burdened with a number of poor people and orphans. The illustration given of these old minutes includes in it the following:—" July 12, 1659—The Session ordains Andrew to go to James Smyth and his wife to debar them from sitting any longer in Wm. Smyth's seat except it be with his own concent." All this ado about seats may be attributable to Cromwell's having used the church of St. Michael to stable the horses of his dragoons, and the fashion that came into vogue of having fixed sittings in presbyterian places of worship.

Aug. 19.—The Session desyred the minister to intermitt the weekly (week day) sermon during the tyme of harvest, and to intimate nixt Sabbath day. Sept. 3, Satterday—Robert Dowglas in Fisherraw became cautioner under the paine of 20 lib., that there shall be no feast made on Charles Hog's child's christening, it being a fast day on the Sabbath. Sept. 24—Compeared Thomas Cathie and Helen Cathie's son for carrying burdens upon the Sabbath day, also Margt. Lowthian compeared for that samine. The Session desyred the minister to rebuke them. They promise never to do the lyke again, being sorie for the doing of it. Nov. 4.—Wm. Rig of Carbarrie elected ruling elder to the Synod. Dec. 25.—Compeared Wm. Younger in Fisherraw, and is ordained to stand in sackcloth the first and last day. Neither his offence or whether the said William did penance is recorded, nor what first or last day as here used meant. Dec. 11—Compeared Geo. Kid, Robt. Forbairne and James Mill, young boys in Smeiton, delated for playing att the buoulls (marbles) on the Sabbath day. They deny the same and are ordained to be heir this day 14 days. They appear on the 25th, are rebuked and promise it will not occur again.

1661, January 27.—The names of the elders were intimate out of the pulpitt, and if there was any that had anything to object against their admission they were to come to the Session before Tuesday nixt and make the Session acquaint ye w^h. Jan. 24.—The qlk day the elders formerly nominat were present, and taken sworn were admitted, nothing being objected against them. June 11.— The minister related the ordinance of the presbytery of Edinburg in relation to the reading in the Church, that they had ordained reading to be by the precentor, a certain space before the incoming of the minister. June 25.—Elspeth Bettson appears, charged with blasphemy " in saying God is not a righteous God in taken away my husband." She denied this, bot only confest and said "what could God do more to me." At two subsequent meetings witnesses were examined on oath in reference to this charge, and it was then remitted to the presbytery. The poor broken-hearted widow could hardly find consolation in this method of dealing, or the more likely learn that the Lord loveth those he chastens.

Nov. 5, 1661.—The Session and the baillies desyred the minister to mak intimation out of the pulpitt anent Janet Stoddart, who was imprisoned upon the suspicion of witchcraft, that if any people has any thing to lay to her charge they was considerably to come w'n ten or twelve dayes, other ways they would Dimitt her, in regard she was great expense to the Magistratts.

1661, Dec 29.—The Session think fitt that everie Sabboath day in the collecting of the poor folks' money that there be an elder waiting on to help to collect w^t ane other ordinary man, in respect it is reported that the vulgar sort of people without authority distributts the collections to several persuns who attend at the porch and style neidlesslie.

Corroborative of the antiquity of St. Michael's of Inveresk are such entries as these: Sept. 30, 1666.—The qlk day the Session being weiil convened after intimation out of the pulpitt for repairing of the ruins of the fabrick of the kirk which is above Craigmillar's yle, they did elect some of their number to meet upon it and to take cognisance of the samine how it should be best repaired. Oct. 20, 1668.—It was motioned "that the timber of the steeple is fayling," and a workman was ordered to be employed to "view it." Again

May 29, 1677, two hundred merks expended on finishing the steeple as also for poynting the body of the church with sklates (slates) and lime where there had been great need of, and a committee is appointed to fix what proportion of the expenditure each heritor had to pay. The appointment of a special week-day service served to provide an opportunity for the celebration of marriages in church, for which there were certain dues to be applied to the relief of the poor. The desire to be singular made itself conspicuous even in this, and on Mar. 12, 1667, the Session put those parties who sought to be different from other people on the higher level for which they longed, and ordained them to be charged twentie pounds Scots money for the use of the poor. Complaint had been made even earlier that newly married couples were escorted to the kirk by multitudes of people, and their kirking was made the occasion of feasting, " which was to be thought upon att lengthly."

1670, March 20.—John Wilson, George Dreddon, and Alex. Smart, Skipperers in Fisherrow, made an application for sittings on behalf of the rest of their incorporation, which was granted upon a payment for the behoof of the poor, and to be the first of the Fisherman's Loft. It must have been in a dark corner, for on 22 Feb. 1676, "a window to the Seaman's loft is condescended to."

Nov. 8, 1674.—It was intimate out of the pulpitt be the minister, that those who are able and yitt give nothing in to the brod for the use of the poor, that they amend it heirafter. If the shortcomings of those able to give were thus pointedly proclaimed, an equally sharp eye was kept on the receivers of poor's money. June 22, 1675.—The qlk day it is ordained, according to ane former act, that those within the parish who goes a begging from house to house should only geit half a merk a month, and those that goes not to have a merk. The parishioners were much pestered with beggars coming from a distance, and to distinguish the local poor all of them who asked for alms were ordered by the Session to wear a badge upon their breast. Oct. 24.—James Richardson, younger, of Smeaton, in respect of his father's inability, Sir Adam Blair, younger, of Carbarrie, and Alexander Hay of Monktoun were proposed and approved for the eldership. The minister called attention to the large number of parishioners who were ill with bloody flux and in a starving condition: that the sums received at the church doors were inadequate to meet present necessities, and proposed that a charge of 40 shillings be made upon those who desired to have the church bell rung at the time of funerals as was done in other parishes. This was agreed to. Another expedient to increase the poor's money was a levy made for permission to erect grave stones

MEMORIAL STONE WHERE QUEEN MARY SURRENDERED.

" with lettering." But even when pinched to make ends meet, practical help was extended to others beyond the parish. Dec. 28, 1675.—A contribution of £11, 10s. was made by the landward, and £29, 17s. 10d. by the burgh for the brunt houses at Newbattle.

Feb. 1, 1676.—The qlk day there was a letter sent to Mr Rob. Jossy to produce a testimonial from the next kirk parish, called St. Cuthbert's kirk, under the minister's hand, etc. This affords an idea how large an area Inveresk had included at that date.

May 2, 1676.—In intimating the Communion the elders are desyred be the Minister to reconcile people who are known to be at variance. At one time a collection was made for the people of Glasgow, at another for Kilmarnock, for Ormiston, for Newbattle, for a bridge at Coldstream, for the repair of Peterhead harbour, for poor people burnt out of their homes in Newbigging.

These contributions were ordered to be made by the Session, Presbytery, Synod, Privy Council or Parliament.

Chapter XIII.

PARISH FINANCE—XVII. CENTURY.

THE careful attention given to the administration of monies entrusted to Kirk-Sessions for the use of the poor, and to the general finance of the parish, is well seen in a volume of accounts which cover the fourteen years from 1655 to 1669. In these a regular system of book-keeping is followed, and the receipts and disbursements are set down distinctly. Towards the close of each year new Treasurers were elected by the Session for the landward and burghal portions of the parish, who entered upon office as on the first of January, but did not intromit with any monies till an audit of the preceding treasurers' books had been made. At these audits an abstract of the retiring treasurers' accounts was drawn up and recorded, followed by an enumeration of the securities for money at interest, and all else for which the newly appointed treasurers would be held responsible. For example, at the installation of treasurers for 1665 on January 19

it is thus entered :—Burgh Compts. Imprimus
Johne Smart, Thesaurer, is charged with ye collections for ye poore for ye year 1654, w^ch
extends to . . 286 lib. 12 8
It w^t penalties, pands esigned and
lost and annual rents, extends to
the soume of . . 182 lib. 2 0
Summa of his charge is . 468 lib. 14 8
His discharge, given out for supplying ye poore for ye year 1654
extends to . . 364 lib. 14 0
It for repairing ye kirk which was
summed, at ye easter loft, ye pillar
of repentance, the place for baptisms . . 90 lib. 0 0
Summa is . . 454 lib. 14 0
So rests of frie money, which the
said Johne is to give in to Richard
Calderwood, Thesaurer for ye year
1655 the soume off . 14 lib. 0 8
It ye said Johne Smart delyvered to
Rich^d. Calderwood ye Thesaurer
as follows :—
Imprimus of superplus of his compts. 14 lib. 0 8
Then comes list of bonds, &c., headed with (1) Ane
obligation granted be the toun of Mussilb^h of borrowed money of Jaj mks, ye date Januar 9, 1643.

In the corresponding vidimus of the landward
accounts only 157 lib. 6, 4, is shown to have

been required for the relief of the poor, being less than half what the burgh had had to distribute. For the second item of discharge, this treasurer has pands esigned at the marriage redelyvered . . 11 lib. 9 0 and for the third, a duplication of the burgh's payment for the repair of the Kirk . 90 lib. 4 0 Among the obligations handed over is, a note be Robt. Nemmo, Thos. Forman, Ro^t. Douglas, Robt. Vernor, Younger, to the Kirk thesaurer for advancing of 240 lib. w^h was payed to ane English troup, w^h they obliged themselves to repay. Subsequent entries make it clear that this money was used to rid the landward part from a threatened quartering of an English troop upon it. On folios of the account-book the collections at the Church are seen, those to the credit of the burgh on one page, those for the landward on the opposite. The names of the elders who "waited upon the collection" are stated, and the amount received is summed up monthly. Into this branch of the accounts the penalties exacted for certain delinquencies are entered. In another part "pands," and charges for "non-compearance" are separately accounted for. Immediately after the folios first mentioned detailed lists of the recipients of poor's money are given, and payments otherwise chargeable are also included under the respective headings of Burghal and Landward. A wide latitude was taken in dealing with the necessitous. Some payments appear altogether insufficient, others quite generous. All taken together point to the period having been one of hard pinch and much suffering. Some may be taken as examples. Of the local poor, Helen Paterson receives £1, 4s.; Jas. Cowan, £2. Of course Scots money is to be understood. Wm. Cook gets £1, 10s.; Elspeth Gledstanes, 13s. 4d.; Mr. John —— his wyfe, 6s.; Elizabeth Blackhall, £2; blind Barbara Hardie, 13s. 4d.; a cripple, 4s.; another, to buy a barrow, 14s.; Elspeth Merstoun, who was long lying and was never helped, £5, 12s. 8d.; a poor man marked M'Kay at the Bridgend, £1, 9s.; two orphans in the Westpannes, £1; an Englishman's wyfe in Newbigging, £1; for a cott to a poor boy, £2; to Christian Thomson who had the brunt house, £6. There are repeated payments for winding-sheets and for the interment of the poor. £4 was paid for Jennet Crawford's winding-sheet, and for some "pack" to make a winding-sheet £2, and Rachel White and her three lame bairnes had £1, 10s; Jas. Harret for himself and his winding-sheet £2, 5s. 4d. The latter is singular, unless it be understood that Jas. felt so concerned about his decent burial his winding-sheet was procured beforehand, to put him at rest regarding a matter long regarded as a sacred duty among the Scottish peasantry. Payments to casual and outside poor present a curious diversity. Jas. Lindsay is paid £2, 18s. for curing a distracted boy at Inveresk. A captain who was in the king's service receives 24s.; a gentleman 30s.; a stranger riding on a horse, 4s.; a gentleman named Maxwell, 58s.; a stranger who had a recommendation, 18s.; another from the north, who apparently had none, gets 24s.; one deposed minister receives £5, another £1; 12 shipbroken men get 12s.; 2 Frenchmen that were shipbroken, 8s.; 26 seamen who were robbed, for meat and drink, 32s.; 4 Frenchmen, 30s.; 4 Dutchmen, 12s.; 5 sodgers, 10s.; 2 cripple sodgers, 24s.; a sodger that came from France, 8s.; a soldier that is mutilatt, 12s.; a gentleman at Carbarrie's desire, £3; an Englishman, a traveller, 6s.; an English gentleman, £4: an Englishman that had a printed pass, £2, 18s.; a stranger, Wm. Murray, £6; a poor woman that came from Dundee, 12s.; a stranger from Dumfries, 20s.; while a poor woman from Tweedmouth gets 6s.; a stranger in the Queensferry, 6s.; and a man with a plaid and poor woman must be content with half of it. Perhaps the plaid and poor woman were thought an equivalent for the difference. "A cripple transporting" often occurs, that is sending him on to the next parish that he may not become a permanent burden. Stranger folk did not fare badly. A passenger scholar receives 32s.; three strangers, 30s.; a gentleman at the Presbytery, 58s.: David Ferguson, who had a recommendation from the Estates, £6; but one who came out of Argyle, only 6s.; Thomas Wood and his wife in Dalkeith, 24s.; one in Ormiston, who is infected with disease, £6; Helen Dobie, for quartering strangers, is paid £4, 8s.; and the constable at Monktonhall, for quartering several French sodgers, 6s. Laurence Forrest, to give his son, gets £4; Wm. Brown, bursar, son to Henry Brown, has £20 one half-year; and Archbald Gowrlaw, for John Gay's prentisse, £24. £12, 9s. was given 27 Nov. 1655 "for the burning at Edinburgh to mak up the 400 merks."

Of payments connected with the kirk, a woman for cleaning it gets 6s., a book to hold the names of those who died, cost £1, a Psalm Book, 16s., Kirk Bible for minister's use and "examine book," £14. Costly books these! Paper for long and short compt[s] £1, 4s., Adam Grinlaw for 200 tickitts £1, 6s. 8d., a letter carrying 4s., a key to the trance door 6s., a key to the offering house door, north style 6s., mending key of steeple and others 24s., water basin for the baptisms, Nov. 1659, £2, 8s., a glass window to the seats behind John Cathie's seat 36s., glass window to the Wester loft £7, 16s.; repairing Wester window, the Wester loft door, snecks and locks and the North style mending £4, 11s., glass for Session House £7, 4s., 2 Tirlays for the Wester loft window £3, 4s., a window in

Craigmillar's yle mending £1, 2s., mending the North kirk style which was spoiled with rain 13s. 4d., mending it again 6s., helping the furmes in the North style 12s., mending the kirk gavel 18s., timber and work to South style £8, 8s., lime for the kirk dyke £1, 4s., towes to the bell 3s. That is more economical than splicing the bell-rope. The slater however had a heavier account. A hundred sklaites to the kirk cost £4, 10s., more for carrying them £1, 15s. 8d., lyme and sand £3, 6s.; George Thomson for his work to the kirk "wh his drinks" £9, 14s., more for nails 18s., mending the sarking 6s., a nice little bill of £20, 9s. 8d. At the time to which these accounts belong, the kirk had a source of income from the Justices of the Peace. All that is stated about it is, "Given by the justice of the peace of the burgh, or of the landward." In 1660 from the former £48, 3s. was received, from the latter £30. Whether from this cause or some other, the Magistrates and Heritors came by-and-bye to wish to examine the kirk treasurer's accounts as well as the Session, and the question was taken before the Presbytery which decided, 30th June 1702, "that they may be present to satisfy any doubts or jalousses they may pretend to have, but that the Session are the proper judges in these matters." In that decision all parties acquiesced.

On 27 June 1665, a payment of £13, 6s. 8d. to

the minister for preaching in the Tolbooth, the only one of its kind happened upon, indicates that even the inmates of "droopsey" as a portion of the old burgh jail was called, had at least some consideration shewn them by the parish minister.

Chapter XIV.

CLOSE OF XVII. CENTURY.

MOMENTOUS changes were witnessed in the period with which the two preceding chapters deal. Puritanism and profligacy had in turn their swing, Presbyterianism and Episcopacy their innings. When the Rev. Oliver Colt began his ministry Charles I. was king and the patronage of Inveresk was in his gift. But when Roundheads gained the ascendency, Monarchy and Cavalier had to bow their heads, till another turn of the kaleidoscope recalled Charles II. to sit upon his father's throne. While State affairs thus underwent revolution, and Monarchy, Commonwealth, and Restoration had each their turn, the parish of which Mr. Colt had oversight was not outside the whirl. The memorable sittings of the Westminister Assembly in the Jerusalem Chamber began two years after his settlement. To its sessions, extending over five years, have to be ascribed the Confession of Faith, the Shorter Catechism and the metrical version of the Psalms which are Scotland's heritage. Lord Lauderdale, an heritor of Inveresk, and lord of the lordship of Musselburgh, sat in that august meeting, as one of the elders elected to share in its proceedings by the Church of Scotland. It can hardly be uncharitable to class his lordship with those who were Presbyterian for the sake of plunder, or Prelatic when it served their purpose. The inscription placed upon his monument in Inveresk Church lauds him loudly: history paints his character in other colours. With this fawning courtier and fanatic persecutor pastor and parishioners had to do. From him the burgh received one of its charters, which fittingly contains express power to put accused to inquisition, to inflict torture to extort incrimination. The pressure of his iron hand can be seen where the record of church life is abruptly broken.

During the troubles of 1645 the minister of Inveresk had a protection from the celebrated Montrose, and when Cromwell took possession of his residence he sought shelter in Dundee. On the closing day of the year 1660 he probably witnessed the meeting of the Earl of Middleton with the nobles and others who had horses, at Musselburgh, which must have been reckoned a great affair by all with monarchal leanings, for as Nicoll's account has it, " the town of Edinburgh met him there."

But, everybody did not regard all this trouble and trial seriously ; and so Grant tells of a curious foot-race, to be run by sixteen fishwives from Musselburgh to the Canongate Cross for twelve pairs of lamb's harrigals, in 1661, of which intimation appeared in one of the papers of the period. This exhibition of athletics may have been harmless enough in itself, and the nymphs of many petticoats may have enjoyed the fun, the winner even have been proud of her prize; but it may be taken to indicate a wild rebound from the strictly decorous conduct for which minister and elders had vainly striven.

At London very different business was on foot. Presbyterianism had been banned, Episcopacy had been blessed, and a batch of bishops for Scotland received their consecration in Westminster Abbey. Tytler tells that they made a triumphal entry into Edinburgh on their return with a numerous retinue, including many needy waiters upon Providence, and we learn from John Nicoll that, the Archbishops of St. Andrews and Glasgow, and the Bishop of Galloway, were received with great reverence and pomp at Musselburgh on Tysday, 8 Apryll 1662.

With these historical facts in view, it must be considered creditable to the steadfast adherence of Mr. Colt to his convictions that, onwards to 7 Aug. 1677, when he had reached his eightieth year, the minutes of his Session go on without a break, and their cessation at that point may well be attributable to increasing infirmity. It, however, is worth notice that between March 9 and Oct. 1662, only one entry of three lines occurs on July 29 to this effect:—"It was thought fitt be sundrie elders that the weekly sermon should be intermitt during the tyme of harvest." Mr. Colt died 30 Dec. 1679 in his 82nd year and 48th of his ministry. He was a burgess and Guild Brother of the City of Edinburgh, and left one son who became solicitor to the king. Before passing from the records of a ministry at an eventful time, notice may be taken of two parishioners of note connected with the parish church. Besides Lord Lauderdale and Lady Dunfermline already mentioned, the Earl of Haddington occupied Newhailes, and his name incidentally occurs in the minutes. Sir, afterwards, Lord William Sharpe, son of the Archbishop murdered on Magus Moor, resided at Stoneyhill, and with reference to him the following is of interest:—Jan. 29, 1677. The qlk day it was represented to the minister and the Session that Sir Wm. Sharpe desyred to have the use of the loft above the north style for the better accommodation and convenience of himself and his family betwixt sermons at the noontyde of the day, the whole members of the Session that were present condescended to his desyre save only the two Communion Lord's Dayes in which they were to mak use of them their selfes. To one of Mr. Adam

Colt's elders attention has been called in a remarkable manner. When it became necessary to excavate to a considerable depth to find a solid foundation for the Organ Chamber in the early months of the present year, an elaborately sculptured tombstone was disinterred. Of its reverse side we give an illustration. It is now placed in the entrance lobby of the church. Once cleaned, it was ascertained to be in memory of William Smyth, Clerk of Musselburgh and portioner of Mountainhall. How full the records of the period are is shewn by the details they disclose concerning this personage. He has been ascertained to have been one of the kirk-session, to have acted as a collecting elder, as a server of the tables, as an auditor of the accounts, to have taken his turn as kirk treasurer, to have been an adviser upon questions of difficulty, and to have been Session-Clerk. The inscription "Fidelitis Fecimus" upon his monument, which may be rendered "We have done faithfully," appears to have been well deserved. It will be observed that this William Smyth is described as of Mountainhall. To shew that this spelling of Monktonhall was not unusual, there is an entry in the books of Old Greyfriars' Church Yard bearing that,—"Andrew M'Neill, in Mountainhall, was shot 14 April 1736," that is by the City Guard, under Captain Porteous, at the execution of Andrew Wilson in the Grassmarket. With the installation of a new minister another order is in force. Lauderdale, now Duke, is paramount, and the appointment is given to Arthur Millar, A.M., of Dumbarton, a clergyman reputedly as much distinguished for piety as for his adherence to the Episcopal order. He entered upon his duty at Inveresk 9 June 1680, and continued in its discharge till 3 May 1689, when he preferred to submit to deprivation of his charge, rather than yield obedience to the proclamation of the Estates and pray for William and Mary. In this nominee of the Duke of Lauderdale, the finer features of the period and a conscientiousness of belief make themselves seen, for which those of his way have too often received little credit. Mr. Millar removed to Leith, and became pastor to the Episcopalians there. He was consecrated on 22d Oct. 1718 a bishop without a see, but was appointed to the diocese of Edinburgh in 1727. He died before installation into that office.

For five years following Mr. Millar's expulsion from Inveresk no successor appears to have been appointed. The passing over of the storm is indicated by the way in which the new incumbent received appointment. Richard Howieson, A.M., minister of Cockpen, "was called" 10 Aug., and was admitted to the charge 18 Sept., 1694. He died in Nov. 1700. Of these two incumbencies there are no records.

Chapter XV.

OPENING OF THE XVIII. CENTURY.

AT the commencement of the eighteenth century the Marquis of Tweeddale, Pinkie House, Sir Robert Dickson of Inneresk, Sir James Richardson of Smeatoun, Sir William Binning of Wallyford, and Sir William Sharp of Stoneyhill, were the principal heritors of the landward part of the parish. All these were acquiescing parties to the call given to Mr. John Williamson, son of the Rev. David Williamson of St. Cuthberts, on 14 January 1702. This call was most harmonious, and Mr. Williamson's ordination marked the beginning of a long and faithful ministry. The call was prepared by Mr. Robert Vernor, Town Clerk of Musselburgh, and is engrossed in full in the Minutes. The whole procedure is recorded in detail, the appointment of a Committee of Heritors, Heads of families and Elders to obtain the presbytery's concurrence, that having been obtained, and the edict of the Presbytery appointing the day for Mr. Williamson's ordination to be "Thursday the last day of April instant." No time was lost in entering upon parish business. On the Sunday following his or-

WM. SMYTH'S TOMBSTONE.

dination a meeting of Session was held, "Sederunt Mr. John Williamson our settled minister and the elders." During the first month four meetings of Session took place, at the third of which a Committee was appointed to commune with Sir Robert Dickson of Inveresk anent a colleague to Mr. Williamson. This led to further consultation and an intimation being made from the pulpit on 14 June 1702 "that the Heritors, Magistrates and Elders were to meet that day eight days for getting ane assistant." The need for such help being obtained by Mr. Williamson no one questioned, the only difficulty raised was about the payment, and eventually a tentative arrangement was come to for one year, and Mr. William Dun appointed at a salary of 500 merks, 300 out of the casualties and Session dues. How the other 200 merks were to be raised was left for future deliberation. Having succeeded so far Mr. Williamson and his elders tackled the Heritors and Magistrates about the establishment of a parish school, but could not get them to move; they, therefore, referred the matter to the Presbytery.. A long minute, dated 23rd August, embodies a Presbyterial Act, deposing from the office of the ministry Mr. James Cruickshanks, lately Episcopal incumbent at Douphinston, charged among other things with irregular administration of Gospel ordinances, and which Act was enjoined to be read

L

from the pulpits of Inveresk, Neatoun, Cockpen, and Fala. A new south stile, porch, or collection-house was again required, and the accounts incurred were appointed to be paid: for mason work, fiftie pounds Scots.; for wright work and nails, eight pounds Scots.; and for three pair of bands, and a pair of crooks, and two bolts, seven pounds fifteen shillings Scots.

Immoral conduct must have been very prevalent when Mr. Williamson came to Inveresk, and cases of discipline were frequent. The perusal of such entries presents a painful picture, and the manner of dealing with them appears now more fitted to harden than to lead to penitence and contrition. A curious entry in connection with a case where the delinquent had been compelled to stand on more than one occasion at the church door in sackcloth is met with, Jan. 26, 1703, when the Session is informed he "is taken on to be a soldier and incarcerated to be shipped." April 9, 1704, Margaret Ducat appeared and confessed to the Session that she had been married by an Episcopal minister, from whom she produced a certificate to that effect. All parties concerned, including the two witnesses, were ordered to be referred to the Justices of the Peace. On April 25 twenty-two new elders are nominated, and, no objections being taken, Tuesday, ninth of May, was appointed for their ordination. June 4, 1706, The elders that went through some parts of the paroch in time of sermon reported that they found some people bringing in kail (cabbage) and water, upon which the Session appointed that intimation be made from the pulpitt next Lord's Day that such evil practices may be foreborn hereafter, and particularly that masters of families doe take care that their children and apprentices be kept from profaning the Lord's Day. July 30, 1706, Twelve pounds Scots is sent to help build a harbour at Irvine. A protracted business with a "thrawn" schoolmaster and session-clerk occupied the Session a long time before they could recover minutes made by him on scraps of paper to enable the records to be written up, and forms a subject in many meetings. Dec. 3, 1706, Minister reports that his house had been "broken" by thieves, although the windows had iron staunchions, these having been pressed out, and that several subsequent attempts had been made to effect an entrance. That he had lost a number of valuable things, and had had to keep men watching his house by night in consequence. He offered to be at greater part of the expense, if the Session would sanction "darkening brods and bars for the whole lower story of the manse" and pay the remainder, to which they agreed. At this meeting the non-payment of the Ordination Dinner cropped up, the Session not considering it fit that it should be charged in their accounts, but after explanation

given it was allowed on the express condition that
the treasurer "seek in that money from the
Heritors or any who employed him to make ready
that dinner." On Jan. 21 following, the treasurer
reported his diligence in pressing for payment, but
that he could get no satisfying answer or expecta-
tion that he would be paid. The minister bore this
out, stating he had spoken freely on the subject to
Sir Robert Dickson, to whom he represented that
it was scandalous that he, the patron, who had
taken such a prominent part in calling him to be
minister should not see it paid, since he had
ordered the ordination dinner. But Mr Williamson
fared no better than the treasurer, Sir Robert
telling him he had already paid his share to John
Duncan, writer in Edinburgh, his Baylie; and the
said John Duncan being dead the money had
perished with him. Nothing was consequently to
be done but to authorise payment. Jan. 28, 1707,
This day's collection being nineteen shillings Scots,
is ordered to be given to John Wilson in Carbarrie
and his family, who are in a very indigent condition. The Session at this time had 500 merks, for
which they found great difficulty to obtain a
"sufficient" borrower. On April 20 the Session
desire the minister to buy the Acts of the General
Assembly as soon as he can for their use. From
Sept. 24 to Nov. 15 1707, there were no meetings
of the Session, and a special entry by way of

exculpation attributes this to meeting of presbytery and synod and the minister's indisposition. The collection on the latter date, sixteen pence, is given to John Thomson, a poor man within the paroch. Dec. 9, Ten pounds Scots paid over for the Presbytery's bursar, April 18, 1708. The elders who visited Musselburgh and Ffisherrow this day inform the Session that they saw several young people walking in the streets and fields in time of sermon, wherefore they appoint that intimation be made next Lord's Day from the pulpit that parents and heads of families restrain their servants from profaning the Sabbath, and that people may be seriously dehorted from sitting idle at their doors on the evenings of the Lord's Day. June 8, "The steps where the people ascend to the church on the north syd are quyt wrong (they not having been mended since the Revolution)," the Session resolve to have them repaired as soon as may be, but were afraid the expense would be too burdensome. They, therefore, appointed the minister and the burgh treasurer to wait upon the Magistrates and Town Council to desire them to order the neighbours to give their services and the use of carts and horses for the repair of these steps. In carrying out this instruction a representation was made in writing setting forth the "uneasiness" of the approach and the design of the Session gradually to level it by introducing "several steps of stair," and asked the use of carts "to overlay the even walks between them with gravell." The Magistrates and Council received the deputation graciously, granted their request, and passed an act thereupon. Aug. 26.—Meeting was held with Sir Robert Dickson and Sir Wm. Binning relative to building seats in the body of the church; to this all parties agreed, but before proceeding "they appoint the minister to acknowledge the Duchess of Buccleuch and Marquis of Tweedale and other principal heritors, and likewise that he acquaint the Magistrats of Musselburgh with this design." Nov. 9.—Jean Crombie, relict of Robert Guthrie, schoolmaster in Inveresk, petitions the Session to be put on the poor's roll, being in necessitous circumstances since her husband's death. The Session appoints her to receive twenty shillings Scots a-month, to commence from the beginning of the month, and the minute is expressed in sympathetic terms. On the same day the Session consent to the building of the manse close dyke, considering how inconvenient and dangerous it was to have the minister's house so much exposed, the latter undertaking at the time to advance the cost thereof. How pleasant it is to find such an entry as this, Feb. 7, 1716. The Session here think fitt to observe that though we frequently mett there were no delations or other business that was needful to be recorded, or this on July 3. There have been frequent meetings of the Minister and Elders during this interval but there having been no delations—there was no formall constitute Session needful. These indications of a marked improvement in morals and social conditions, entirely accord with what those historians who have the most attentively studied the question assert to have been the result of an energetic effort to provide for the education of the people. They affirm that in a quarter of a century the difference was remarkable, and here it is seen conspicuously perceptible in the ranks of a community, the constituents of which ranged from the humble peasant to the peer of the realm. Mr. Williamson who helped forward and witnessed this change was a man of singular endowments, of a clear head, ready wit, forward and successful in debate. Possessed of considerable literary ability he published a number of works, and took the position in the Church Courts which his talents qualified him to fill. He died 2d Feby. 1740 in the 38th year of his ministry, aged 60 years.

Chapter XVI.

GLOOM FOLLOWED BY SUNSHINE.

NEXT in succession to Mr. John Williamson the incumbency was held by Mr. Fred. Carmichael, M.A., and his appointment involved the parish in the distraction and discord which lay patronage wrought in the Scottish Church. The gifts and graces which he proved to be possessed of did not avail to make his presentation the less obnoxious. It has been truly said the Church of Scotland has always had a way of her own; and her most faithful sons have ever been the men who might be led but would not be driven. The memorial in which the Elders of 1740 presented their views to His Grace the Duke of Buccleuch on the occasion of a vacancy deserves to be accounted courteous, high-toned, earnest. It was in these terms:—
Memorial to His Grace the Duke of Buccleuch by the Kirk-Session of Inveresk. The peaceable settlement of a duly qualified minister in this parish being a matter of very great importance, and the office of Elder requiring of us that we should contribute our outmost endeavours towards

it, we think it our indispensible duty to lay the following particulars before your Grace in the most dutiful and respectful manner as matters which deserve the greatest attention. The parishioners of Inveresk are so numerous that our late Pastor found it necessary to have an Assistant. The assistant's maintenance depends upon the settlement of a minister who is agreeable to the parishioners as being paid by them. That maintenance is so small that it might rather be increased than diminished, and yet the diminishing of it is the inevitable consequence of settling a minister in the parish who is disagreeable to the generality of the parishioners. Great numbers of our parishioners take so much exception against the ministers who read the act of Parliament from the Pulpits commonly called Porteous's Act, that they industriously decline to hear them when they preach. The settlement then of any such minister in our parish will be greatly prejudicial both to minister and people, especially to the industrious poor who subsist by the collection made at the Church door: It will make way for a seceding meeting-house in the parish, to which those parishioners will resort. They will soon become seceders from the established Church: yea, be riveted in their secession so as never to return to it, and moreover it will become the source of manifold disorders.

Mr. Frederick Carmichael having been mentioned as a proper person to supply our vacancy, the dutiful regards we owe to your Grace on many accounts make us heartily wish that no just exceptions could be made against him. But we are sorry to find ourselves bound in duty to acquaint your Grace, not only that he has read Porteous's Act in the strictest manner and on that account is very unacceptable to great numbers of our parishioners, but moreover, has so weak a voice that some of our number who attended when he preacht at Prestonpans' Kirk could not hear him, although they were not at the greatest distance from the pulpit, whence we conclude with great certainty that he will not be heard in Inveresk Kirk as being much larger than that of Prestonpans, yea, it being the only Kirk in Scotland, perhaps, which necessarily requires a strong clear voice. We do not take it upon us to name any person to your Grace in this Memorial least it should be misconstrued, presuming your Grace has heard of more than one minister who would be acceptable to our Constituents, we beg leave, therefore, only to say that we flatter ourselves your Grace's nomination will meet with no opposition if any minister with an established character is named, against whom none of the objections before mentioned can be made, and at the same time we persuade ourselves that your Grace will steadily keep in view the peace and welfare of the Parish in naming a minister to supply our vacancy. That this memorial may be someway authentick it is by appointment of the Session to be transcribed and signed in name of the Session by Thomas Young, Sess.-Clk. Deput.

The day after this appeal to the patron of the Parish was agreed upon, the Elders having taken a night to sleep over it, had it again read to them and saw nothing to amend or withdraw. It was accordingly directed to be signed and forwarded. But it was disregarded. This shows how the settlement of a minister was managed, July 6, 1740. This day the Session desired that what was done. Munday, 30th of June, in the Meetting in Geor, Inglis, his house be recorded, which is as follows. The elders being called at eleven of the clock forenoon to the fores[d] Thes[rs] house by Baillie Lindsay not being acquainted what they were to do, Mr. Bonaly being present, my Lord Drummore, Sir Robert Dickson, Mr. Grierson, factor for his Grace the Duke of Buccleuch. After prayer, Sir Robert Dickson desired Mr. Grierson to present to the Session a Moderation for a call to Mr. Frederick Carmichael which was accordingly presented and read over, and after reading the same, Sir Robert, &c., insisted that the Elders should sign it, to which they all conjunctly refused.

So inauspiciously was Mr. Carmichael's introduction to the parish heralded, no minute appears

of his ordination or any entry to convey the
impression of his having received a hearty welcome
by his future parishioners. What the Session
feared seems rather to have come about. Mr. Carmichael was not ordained till 15th April following
his presentation, at which date it is recorded a
Committee of the Session had a meeting to tran-
sacte some routine business, but Mr. Carmichael's
name or the important matter of his ordination is
"industriously absent." Three days before the
solemn event " Thomas Brown, one of our Elders,
gave in his demission as being an Elder under
Mr. Carmichael his ministry while here. Likewise
John Mitchell, George Hill and Geor. Inglis ad-
hered to the same."

Before this unhappy business reached its climax
the Session went about its affairs in a very practical way, and one step taken to bring relief to
prevailing distress is creditable alike to them and
to Sir Robt. Dickson. On Nov. 29, 1740, the Session received a letter from Sir Robt. Dickson, the
purport of which can be gathered from the resolution which it led them to take. The minute
narrates that " they, considering the scarcity of
victuall, and hearing that there was victuall to be
gotten in England much cheaper than in Scotland,
the Session therefore have resolved to lay out one
hundred pounds sterling, which is immediately in
the treasurer's hand for buying up the said victuall,

and this day they ordered that their treasurer, Geor. Inglis, to lodge the said hundred pound ster., in Sir Robt. Dickson's hand, that he may lodge in the new Bank of Scotland and take receipt therefor; if need be, they may draw when they please the said sum."

And the Session did impower Sir Robt. Dickson to buy corn to the best advantage for that behoof, and to be accountable to the Session when required and to draw upon the new bank for the foresaid sum when the corns are brought and delivered.

Another meeting was held the following day, at which the treasurer intimated that the Session's instructions had been carried out, and produced Sir Robert's acknowledgment for the money.

May 4, 1741. With the £100, 162 bolls of oats were purchased, and particulars are from time to time entered as to the quantities received and made into meal. The charges for making 13 bolls, the quantity "gristed" at a time, may be interesting to some, charge for kiln bedding, £1, 10s.; the metsters at Leith, 6s.; 3 men for carrying down the oats, 8s.; charges that day the oats were got out of the ship to the man that put them up in the loft, 10s.

Mr. Carmichael left behind him a memorial, in a neatly designed sun-dial upon a pediment in the Manse Garden, on which is inscribed in Latin a motto, meaning, "Time flieth faster than the

East wind." So possibly he found it in his experience with plenty to do and little time to do it in.

He was translated to New Greyfriars' Church, Edinburgh, 1 Dec. 1747, upon a presentation made by the Town Council of the city.

The last entry previous to his leaving Inveresk is in his own handwriting and authenticated by his signature, in which grateful acknowledgment is made of the faithfulness and diligence of Mr. Arch. Handasyde, treasurer, who the Session re-elect and continue in said office.

Mr. Carmichael's election to another charge is never noticed.

From the City Records it appears he was called to be minister of New Greyfriars, May 4, 1747, in succession to Mr. Jas. Stevenson, translated to Old Greyfriars on April 15, but whose entry thereto was suspended till the vacancy so created is supplied. On 30 July 1752 Mr. Geo. Kay, minister of the Gospel at St. Cuthbert's, called unanimously to be minister of the New Greyfriars in place of the deceased Mr. Frederick-Carmichael, his stipend to be paid out of the City's Duty of 2 Pennies on the Pint. From the same source the cost of building the church and providing its communion plate came. In so expending its revenue the city simply implemented one of the conditions upon which it obtained right to impose this tax on ale.

Chapter XVII.

MINISTRY OF DR. CARLYLE.

ON the morning of the Battle of Prestonpans a young man of twenty-three, an Ex-Edinburgh Volunteer, was taken captive by the Highlanders. Managing to escape he betook himself to the belfry of the parish Church, and from that advantageous position beheld the fight and the rout of the royal forces. That young man was Alexander Carlyle, son of the minister of Prestonpans. Three years later he became minister of Inveresk. He studied at Glasgow, Edinburgh and Leyden and used the opportunities these universities provided to good purpose. The position he was able to take in social circles, among distinguished literati in church courts made him widely known, but did not prevent him discharging his proper functions. Parish memories of him are still cherished and passed on. Older folks at the beginning of the present reign had many traits to tell regarding him, and he was spoken of with unfeigned admiration. And little wonder. If a man may be judged by the company he keeps and the companionships he forms, Carlyle's memory will not suffer eclipse the more these are inquired after. In his "Autobiography," the very features in his character many lament the absence of, he has studiously left unlimned. He does not tell that he was one of the very earliest enrolled members of the Select Society, his name being ninth on the list. That society met in the Advocates' Library every Wednesday evening at six o'clock, from 12 Nov. to 12 Aug., and adjourned its sittings punctually at nine. It was not a society for jollification, but for the discussion of any subject except such as had regard to Revealed Religion, or was concerned with the principles of Jacobitism. It consisted of Peers of the Realm, Judges of the Court of Session, Professors of Edinburgh and Glasgow Universities, Clergymen, Physicians, Surgeons, Advocates, Architects, Writers to the Signet, Officers in the Army, Merchants, and private gentlemen. Of its one hundred and nine members it may safely be said by far the larger number deservedly rank as distinguished Scotsmen. This information regarding the society is taken from a manuscript copy of its Roll and Rules.

In 1760 Mr. Carlyle was nominated to preach before the Lord High Commissioner, a recommendation which stirred up opposition, but after all was agreed to without a vote. It is the only case where objection has been taken in like circum-

Rev. Alex. Carlyle, D.D.

stances. In the following year he received his degree of Doctor of Divinity. In Aug. 1762 he was appointed Almoner to the king, and on 2 July 1785 gazetted one of the Deans of the Chapel Royal. He was Moderator of the General Assembly, May 1770.

In the Charter Chest of the Kirk Session there has been preserved a collection of papers in the Doctor's handwriting, narrating the steps taken by him and his Session in 1790, to establish Sunday Schools in Musselburgh and Fisherrow. It is to be remembered that such schools were regarded with the greatest suspicion and dislike by many of the churchmen of that period. It is matter of history that to such a length was this feeling entertained, some ministers threatened their parishioners with deprivation of church ordinances if they permitted their children to attend these schools, no matter how earnest and godly the teacher or teaching might be. Not so, however, did the clear-headed, dignified, and genial Dr. Carlyle act. He had the penetration to see the influence for good these might be made to wield, and he set himself to the task of modelling his own upon the most advantageous plan that his fertile resources, and the counsel of his friends, could devise.

In this matter, Dr. Carlyle appears in a light which must be almost a revelation to those whose estimate of his private character, ministerial fitness, and pastoral diligence has been formed from a study of his autobiography only, and proves him to have had a high sense of the duties of his sacred office, combined with a keen enjoyment of good living, as then understood, and an intense relish for intellectual pleasures.

From these interesting papers, we make selection of the following *minute*, written on the first page of a sheet of foolscap paper in neat, distinct, and firm handwriting, by Dr. Carlyle himself, and duly authenticated by his signature, and bearing on the back the titling, " Proposal for Sunday Schools." It is in the following terms :—

" Inveresk, August 1st, 1790.

" At this sederunt, the Following Proposal was laid before the Session by the Moderator—

" That whereas it has been Found from experience That Many of the Children of the Lower Rank in this Parish, Tho' they have learn'd to Read in their Infancy, yet Thro' negligence, or their Being early engag'd in some Business, are in Danger of Entirely forgetting what they have been Taught.

" And whereas the New School for Teaching Young Girls a branch of Manufacture, However usefull in other Respects, necessarily occupies all their time in week Days, and makes it Impossible for them to attend Masters for Reading and the Principles of Religion.

"And whereas Multitudes of Children of both sexes are allow'd to Run about Idle the Whole Lord's Day, which tends to Breed them not only in Ignorance, but to Irreverence for Religious Institutions, and consequently to Dissolute Manners, It is Thought That a Sunday's School or two in this Parish, which have been found of so much use in Populous Towns, will help to correct Those abuses, and to prevent these Evils;

"It is therefore propos'd, That an attempt shall be made immediately to form such an institution.

"The same Day, The Session Having taken the above proposal into their Serious consideration unanimously agreed thereto, and Resolved to send Subscription Papers to such Persons as may be able and willing to promote Such a Pious undertaking, That an annual sum may be rais'd, to pay Sallaries to two Masters, one in Musselburgh and another in Fisherrow, and to Defray all other charges that may be necessary.

"ALEX. CARLYLE."

It is deserving of notice that this Minute so carefully drawn and so clearly expressed is thus duly signed, in contra-distinction to the long observed use and wont of allowing the minutes entered in the minute-book to remain without the authentication of the Moderator's signature.

The next indication of the Doctor's zeal and activity in carrying forward this scheme, is a letter or note from Lady Hailes, as follows:—"Lady Hailes's Compts. to Dr. Carlyle, she was sorry she had not the pleasure of seeing him yesterday but could not get away from a Gentleman who had come on business to Lord Hailes, who not being very well was not come out of his room while the Dr. stay'd.

"Lord Hailes approves greatly of the Sunday's School as everyone must, who considers the miserable consequences of the want of instruction to Children. It would be still better if the Funds would allow of a *dayly* school for those Children that are not engaged in work through the week.

"At Lord Hailes's desire Lady Hailes has subscribed £5, 5s.—Newhailes, Sept. 9th."

In this movement Dr. Carlyle was generously supported by the larger heritors, the Duchess of Buccleuch having given annually £10; Lord and Lady Hailes, and latterly Lady Hailes and Miss Dalrymple, £5, 5s.; Lady Hope, £3, 3s.; Mrs. and the Misses Fisher, £5, 5s.

Such is a pleasant glimpse these holograph papers afford of a side of Dr. Carlyle's character little realised. It affords a picture which shews that even a Moderate might have grains of goodness in him, and not be so devoid of a sense of duty and of willingness to work in a good cause as some superior people would sometimes foolishly wish us to suppose.

In Dr. Carlyle's time the old church was in a very ruinous condition and altogether inadequate for the requirements of the community. He had to fight for a dozen years before he got the heritors to undertake the building of a new one, but did not live to take part in the opening of it. He died Aug. 25, 1805, and was buried beside the spot where he had so long laboured.

Chapter XVIII.

THE PRESENT PARISH CHURCH.

ON Friday, 16 Sept. 1803, the corner-stone of the Parish Church was laid with masonic, military, and religious ceremonial. In the official programme of that day's proceedings it is styled The New Church of St. Michael's, Inveresk. Lodge Mussleburgh Kilwinning, convened in the Town Hall at noon, numerous deputations attended to testify their interest in the event, and a number of the local incorporated trades turned out and swelled the assemblage. When all had gathered a procession was formed, and the Masons having proceeded to their Lodge in Dambrae the initial requisite to what was to follow was in due order observed. This building was the oldest in Scotland then associated with Freemasonry. It still remains with the attendant emblems intact, but is no longer the meeting-place of the brethren.

Thence the procession took its way to the church in the following order:—

1st. The Magistrates and Council, attended by their officers with insignia of office and a military band.

THE PRESENT PARISH CHURCH. 183

2nd. The Engineers and architect.
3rd. The Grand Tyler.
4th. The Grand Steward.
5th. The Golden Compass, Square, Plumb, and Level.
6th. The Golden Mallet.
7th. The Cornucopia filled with oats, a silver cup filled with wine, and another filled with oil.
8th. A large crystal Vase containing Medals, Coins, &c., an Edinburgh Almanac (1801), one ditto (1803), in which last is written the names of the officers in the Volunteers of Mussleburgh, an Edinburgh Newspaper of the 13th Sept. 1803, and also a large brass plate on which is engraved the following inscription:—

ST. MICHAEL'S, INVERESK, OF GREAT ANTIQUITY.

The Foundation Stone of this Rebuilt Church was laid on the 16 day of September in the year of Our Lord 1803, in the 43d year of the Reign of Our most Pious and Gracious Sovereign George the Third, and in presence of the Right Worshipful Charles Stewart, Master of the Fraternity of Freemasons of the Kilwinning Lodge in Mussleburgh.

In the Year of Masonry 5803.

Right Worshipful Charles Stewart, Grand Master (late Magistrate).
Alexander Vernor. Depute-Master.
John Taylor, Senior Warden.
Martin Begg, Junior Warden.
David Gullan, Treasurer.
John Kemp, Secretary.
Robert Moir, Grand Steward.
His Grace Henry Duke of Buccleugh, Patron.
Francis Charteris Weemys, Earl of Weemys. ⎫
The Honble. William Elphinstone of Carberry. ⎪
Sir John Hope of Craighall. ⎬ Heritors.
John Wauchope of Edmistone. ⎪
Miss Christian Dalrymple of Hailes. ⎪
Robert Finlay Esqr. of Wallyford. ⎭
In the 56 Year of the Ministry of the Rev. Alexander Carlyle, D.D.
Alexander Clark and George Young, Bailies.
Martin Begg, Treasurer, Mussleburgh.
Messrs. Paton & White, Builders; Robt. Nisbet, Architect.

And to defend our Happy Country against an Invasion at this time, threatened by our Inveterate

THE PRESENT PARISH CHURCH. 185

Enemies, there is now encamped on the Links, under the command of General Sir James St. Clair Erskine, Bart.—North British Militia.

Edinburghshire—Col^{l.} His Grace Henry Duke of Buccleugh.

Dumfriesshire—Col^{l.} Right Honble. The Earl of Dalkeith.

Forfarshire—Col^{l.} The Honble. Archbald Douglas.

Renfrewshire—Col^{l.} Right Honble. The Earl of Glasgow

Next followed the Grand Officers, after whom came Brother Nisbet, senior, carrying the Holy Bible open, on a Velvet Cushion, immediately in front of the Grand Master, with the Duke of Buccleugh on his right and General Sir James St. Clair Erskine, Bart., on his left.

Members of the Lodge, Deputations, and public bodies invited, brought up the rear.

The Stone was placed at the North-East Corner of the building in accordance with the customary order and ceremony observed on such occasions.

The Grand Master in turn addressed the Duke of Buccleugh, Lord of Inveresk and Musselburgh and Patron of the Parish—The Magistrates of the burgh and the venerable minister of the parish, each of whom suitably replied.

Three military bands accompanied the procession and the flank companies of the camp furnished a guard of honour.

The ceremonial at the Church over, Divine Service was conducted in the Burgess Chapel, Newbigging, by Rev. Dr. Carlyle "in a manner suitable to so solemn an occasion."

During the rebuilding of the parish church this dissenting chapel was placed at the service of the congregation of the parish church, a kindness which minister, elders, and people appreciated, and which deserves to be remembered. By a gift to the Minister and Session of the chapel and a handsome gratuity to its church-officer the Session of Inveresk endeavoured to give expression to their gratitude; while the personal esteem in which the minister and his lady were held, received acknowledgments that are still cherished as heirlooms in their family. Dr. Carlyle's letter to the Rev. Alex. Black was in the following terms:

"Manse, Mussh., July 16, 1803.

"REVD. AND DEAR SIR,—I have the satisfaction herewith of transmitting to you and your Session from the Session of the Parish of Inveresk, a Laver or Baptismal Bason, for the use of your Chapel, of which we beg your acceptance."

"The Frank Goodwill with which you offer'd us your Chapel for assembling those of the Establish'd Church for Publick Worship, for a part of every Lord's Day, while the Parish Church is Rebuilding, Demanded some lasting mark of acknowledgment from us, And it is our Special Wish and Prayer to Almighty God that you may Long Continue to exercise your Holy Function, with the same Respect and Success which you have hitherto enjoy'd.

"The Publick Danger now so Imminent Diminishes in a great Degree, to nothing almost, any small Differences in opinion, that may be between us, and magnifies those Many essential Points in which we agree, and Tends to Lessen our Distance from each other.

"In one important Christian Grace That of Benevolence and Brotherly Love, we are of one accord. In this you have lately made the advance, and set us an Example, which has excit'd in us a Mutual Regard which I trust will never cease.

"This I write in my own name and in that of the Session of Inveresk, with every kind wish for Temporal and Spiritual Blessings to you and all your Flock.—I am, with sincere esteem, Revd. and Dear Sir, Your affectionate Brother and most humble Servt.,

"ALEXR. CARLYLE."

Chapter XIX.

DR. MOODIE'S AND MR. BEVERIDGE'S MINISTRIES.

FOLLOWING Dr. Carlyle, the Rev. Leslie Moodie, D.D., Minister of Kelso, was presented to the living. Singularly enough he was ordained to the office of the Ministry by him whom he was to succeed. On his appointment to Newton, Dr. Carlyle presided at the ordination, Mar. 25, 1769, and preached from Heb. VII., 10-25. When minister of that parish, Dr. Moodie made a careful list of all the parishioners, and after his transference to Inveresk, he took the same method of making himself acquainted with his people. In the list so made, church connection and other particulars were carefully noted. He was a gentleman of culture, but never robust, and won the esteem of his flock by the display of abilities essentially different from Dr. Carlyle's, but none the less solid and practical. Dr. Moodie pursued the course in relation to Sunday Schools on which Dr. Carlyle entered, and in 1815 was the only member of Dalkeith Presbytery who had one. A minute of the Presbytery, Apr. 25 of that year bears "there are no Sunday Schools within the bounds of the presbytery, except one at Musselburgh, which is under the inspection and patronage of the minister of that parish." In 1832, Dr. Moodie obtained the services of the Rev. J. G. Beveridge as assistant, who was unanimously chosen by the congregation to be Assistant and Successor when, in 1836, the state of Dr. Moodie's health rendered that step necessary. Dr. Moodie died in 1840. When Mr. Beveridge entered upon the duties of the assistantship, the scourge of cholera was making terrible havoc in the lanes and closes of Musselburgh and Fisherrow. With rare devotion and fortitude, the young minister fearlessly visited where doctors were afraid to go, and when remonstrated with upon his hardihood, is said to have replied, "how could I die better than in doing my duty." Fortunately for the parish his life seemed a charmed one, and he was spared for many years of usefulness and honour. From that time onward through four-and-fifty years, the sick and the sorrowing never claimed his services in vain. Upon the day he died, two, who knew him well, bore this testimony to their departed friend.—" While attentive to the many duties which the pastor of a large parish has laid upon him, the late minister of Inveresk will be best remembered for his assiduous attentions to the sick, the dying and the bereaved. Ungrudgingly and unostentatiously he laboured in this sphere, irrespective of rank or denominational distinction; and that these services were not unappreciated by his parishioners was shewn on various occasions, when he was presented with gifts expressive of the esteem and affection of large numbers, many of whom belonged to congregations other than his own." A truer or better deserved tribute was never penned. Of one of these gifts of which mention is thus made but which it is believed has not before been noticed in print, it may be pardonable to tell. As is well known the late Provost Laurie was a medical practitioner, pronounced Liberal, and Free Churchman. Somewhere in the seventies he had a serious illness, and his medical brethren unitedly watched the case and prescribed for it. In its symptoms occasion was seen for grave alarm. The patient himself recognized the danger, and in its presence particularly desired Mr. Beveridge to be called to his bedside. Often before that they had been unable to agree upon many points. Now they were at one. The venerable pastor whose long experience enabled him to judge of the probabilities of life as few could, spoke words of hopefulness and consolation to the strong man laid low, and ministered to him in language every syllable of which was full of meaning.

Throughout that illness these visits were continued. The crisis was passed, the disease subdued, and health restored. Again convalescent, Provost Laurie confided to an Inveresk elder that he had often been a witness to Mr. Beveridge's attentions to the sick poor, but the experience he had himself had of them made him long to make some acknowledgment in any way that might be thought most considerate to Mr. Beveridge's feelings. The Provost was particularly anxious for the elder to set a presentation afoot, to which he offered a handsome contribution with the warmest countenance of his lady. But, when it was represented that the gracefulness of the gift would be incalculably increased if the initiative were taken by himself he willingly fell in with the suggestion, and he and Mrs. Laurie entered into the movement heart and soul. If anything could have added to the pleasure that gift gave, it was the manner in which it was given. Without parade or public ado the Provost and his lady made a call, and quietly placed the sum they had been instrumental in collecting in Mr. and Mrs. Beveridge's hands. For unguarded utterances and impulsive sayings alone, many remember Provost Laurie, but an act like this deserves better than to be forgotten.

In the course of the present year a much respected Justice of the Peace of a Western County, has favoured the author with some reminiscences of many years ago when he resided in Musselburgh. Among these, one of the most touching, is the memory he cherishes of occasions when Mr. Beveridge and he were the alone mourners who followed to the grave the remains of some poor person of whom the great world and the immediate neighbourhood took no account. Now, this J.P. is a U.P., and no more lovely or appropriate wreath of immortelles could be laid upon the grave of the late minister of Inveresk than such a tribute.

In the vigour of manhood, Mr. Beveridge enjoyed a great reputation as a preacher. He was in closest intimacy with many of the leading ministers of the metropolis and frequently officiated in their pulpits. Had he been willing he might easily have obtained a position of greater prominence, but with the people who had called him, he preferred to abide.

In all that concerned the welfare of the parish, he had a concern. Education had in him a warm friend, and he has been known to take uneducated adults in hand, and initiate them into the mysteries of strokes and pot hooks with capital result. To promising youths he was ever a wise counsellor and a helpful guide. Sanitary questions and healthy homes for the people were subjects near his heart. When cholera threatened in 1864-5, he did not think it beside his duty to tell plainly from the pulpit that God's sunshine and pure air were meant to be admitted within men's dwellings

and not to be shut out of them. That it was vain to expect exemption from disease if the feeders of it were kept pestilentially polluting the atmosphere beside the people's dwellings. He knew too well the havoc unhealthy houses make, the lassitude and craving for stimulants that they engender, and the unhappiness and degradation to which they lead. This knowledge impelled him to lend all his influence in support of every scheme prudently undertaken for their improvement, and he thereby strengthened the hands of the authorities when sanitary science was less studied than it is now.

In the earlier days of Mr. Beveridge's ministry, the manner of many at public worship must have been sorely trying. Irreverence was, doubtless, not meant, but little reverence was outwardly visible. The appearance of the Church was hardly calculated to inspire devotional feeling. A great gaunt building, with many pews unoccupied, its woodwork never touched by painter's brush, its walls dingy and dusty, and having a pulpit high-perched and ungainly, surmounted with a crown like canopy on which was an eagle with extended wings, had a chilling rather than an inspiriting influence. Add to this that a common custom of the occupants of adjoining pews was to enter into audible conversation on taking their seats at entry, and, when possessed of a snuff-box to send it on a journey round their acquaintances, and the every-Sunday preparative, thought fitting for worship, is recalled. With such a commencement, it need not be thought strange that the conclusion was in keeping. When the minister rose to pronounce the benediction, it shocked few to see one hand stretched out to lift the hat, and the thumb and forefinger of the other placed upon the bolt with which·every pew door was furnished, that a hasty exit might be made before the last echo of the "amen" had passed away. The dispersion of a congregation in these days was just about as hurried and unceremonious as the "skailing" of a school.

Sensitive in his feelings and possessed of a musical instinct that had been carefully cultivated, Mr. Beveridge was an accomplished flute and violin player, and the harsh and discordant notes that passed for praise must often have distressed his soul. To the improvement of the psalmody he naturally gave heed, and the choir of his Church came to be of repute. With the movement to employ instrumental aids in the service of the sanctuary he early identified himself, and had the satisfaction to find the subject so generally acceptable to his people and heartily supported that a Organ by Conacher of Huddersfield was introduced into Inveresk Church in 1871. Out of a membership then numbering six hundred and sixty-five, three only were found to object to the course proposed, and even these offered no opposition to it being gone on with.

The concluding years of Mr. Beveridge's ministry were uneventful. As his natural vigour lessened the respect in which he was held increased. So long as strength enabled he went about his duties with rare fidelity, and never deputed to another what he could himself undertake. Even when so enfeebled as to be unable for any public appearance he kept session with his elders, and the last meeting held was but ten days before his death. Those who were then present can never forget the solemnity of the occasion. On Sabbath morning, October 6, 1886, the summons came and he entered into his rest.

Chapter XX.

MEMORABLE EVENTS.

WITHIN the compass of the present volume little more can be attempted than to give a rapid outline of interesting events connected with the parish. The battle of Pinkie is a subject upon which much might be written. Of it Tytler, the historian, and Grant, the novelist, have furnished thrilling accounts; Patten, the chronicler, attached to the expedition, has left a wonderfully full description of the locality and of the events of that sanguinary day. His diagrams, although imperfect in some details, are in the main accurate, and enable his narrative to be readily understood, and his story followed. The English army camped before the battle "nye a toune they call Salte Prestoun by ye Fryth," and there one banished out of England gave himself up and "was taken to mercie." Fawside is spoken of as "a sorry castell, and half a score of houses of a lyke worthiness to it." From the English camp the position of the Scots was seen, and its strength apparent. The Scottish army occupied the ridge beyond the river from Campie level crossing onward towards Edmonston, the position being known in earlier times as, Edmonston Edge. Patten describes it thus: In front it had a "ryver called the Esk, running north till the Fryth which y^t was not very depe of water, so wear the banks of it so hie and stepe after ye manner of the Peaths mentioned in our Mundais iourney as a small sort of resistauntes might have been able to kepe down a great number of cummers up. We are warned, if we wear wise of these witless louts by ye commune provurbe that saith, it is better sit still than ryse up and fall, but by lyke they knowe it not." Besides this defence the camp was protected on the south by a great marsh between it and the Esk, and again, between it and the enemy an extensive morass stretched along the hollow below Carberry Hill, which Patten calls the Slough, and across which neither infantry nor cavalry could safely venture. To examine more commandingly the position of the Scots the Duke of Somerset and the Master of the Ordnance took up a position on Carberry Hill. The trenches, then thrown up with their protecting outposts in front, can still be seen. The site chosen by "My Lord Protector's Grace" is marked by an upright slab which is thus inscribed: "These entrenchments were thrown up by the English before the Battle of Pinkie, 10 Sept. 1547."

On the day before the battle the Scottish army left its strong position, defiled across the bridge at

Musselburgh, and prepared to encounter the English in the open field. Over estimating their own strength, a party of horse rashly challenged the enemy, and being completely discomfited prepared the way for the terrible defeat which the Scots experienced when the main struggle came.

The Duke of Somerset's skill was quick to see the advantage he had gained, and changed his own position to a point within the grounds of Eskgrove, from which the entire scene could be surveyed and the movements directed. The spot chosen is at the end of the Long Walk, where a monument has been erected bearing this inscription, "The Protector, Duke of Somerset, encamped here, 9 Sept. 1547." The engagement of the following day was most disastrous to the Scots. Beaten upon the field, they were pursued from it, and within three hours and over a distance of about three miles it was estimated no fewer than thirteen hundred were slain. In telling this tale of slaughter, Patten seems to have been much impressed with the "tallness of stature, cleanness of skin, bigness of bone, and due proportion of parts" that he observed among the Scottish dead. That day was long known as Black Saturday in Scotland, and the English after the battle found on Sunday a welcome rest. Says Patten again, "Sainct Candelmas is masculine, feminine, or neuter sainct. Swete Saincte Sunday ye cums ones a weke." The English, left in possession of the field, gave to their dead the rites of burial, and when in later times the place of interment was discovered Sir John Hope of Pinkie had a coppice planted to mark the spot.

Although the Duke of Somerset proved victorious in this battle the object of the campaign was not achieved, nor was the union of the crowns and kingdoms furthered by his triumph.

Twenty years later within a gun-shot from the spot on Carberry Hill where Somerset looked down on the Scottish host, Mary Stuart practically delivered up her sceptre, and began the progress along that doleful road which led to the block. Despite all the attempts which have been made to extenuate her treatment, to blacken her character, and discredit her faith, her bearing upon the scaffold sheds a lustre upon her name. The place of surrender is marked by an inscribed stone which forms the subject of one of the illustrations.

On the 5th Aug. 1600, what is known as the Gowrie Conspiracy, was enacted at Perth. Amid the rejoicings at the failure of this attempt to secure the person of King James VI., a huge bonfire was lighted upon Fawside Hill. With very different significance its beacon fire was set ablaze on the night of the False Alarm, 31 Jan. 1804. By a blunder of the watchman at Hume Castle the whole of the south of Scotland was dotted with heights sending out a ruddy glare, the pre-arranged signal to tell that the French had landed on British soil. One incident of that eventful night, from the lips of an officer who took part in it, may be worth recording. Mr. Supervisor Duncan, of the Excise, long a much respected parishioner of Inveresk, was at the time a young officer of the Perth City Volunteers. When the distant signal was descried the bugles sounded the Assembly, and when the corps mustered not one man failed to answer the roll-call. Face to face with the realities of war the march was begun, and not till Stirling was reached did they learn that a blunder had been committed, and that they might return to their homes. On 27 Aug. 1714 the pulpit of Inveresk Church was ordered by the Session to be "mounted" with black cloth for mourning for the Queen, and Wm. Paiston, taylor, was not to exceed ten shillings in doing this. Mar's Rebellion, 1715, is thus noticed in a minute of Nov. 15. The which day albeit we have not had meetings for discipline since in this time of the lands confusion as usual, yet we have several times met for prayer and conference, and we think it proper to take notice of the Providence of God, of an ingagement of King George's fforces, under the Duke of Argile, against the Rebells, under the Earl of Mar, upon Sabbath last, the threeteenth instant, near Dumblaine, and of the defeat of the Rebells, but we wait for a more full and particular account thereof.

Of Prince Charlie's passage to and from Prestonpans no notice is taken in the Session Records, but tradition tells of the grace with which he bowed to the fair dames who witnessed his progress by way of the Mercat Gate, and of his having passed one night at Pinkie House.

On the occasion of the visit of George IV. to Scotland great hopes were excited that he would ride from Dalkeith House to the Great Review on Portobello Sands by way of Inveresk, and in anticipation of his coming the Magistrates made befitting preparation. The townsfolk were nothing loath to give the king a proper reception, and the different trade corporations made an excellent display. But, while patiently waiting, the gun-fire which announced his arrival upon the sands also informed them their show was in vain. The ranks hurriedly dispersed, and hastened to Portobello to become spectators of the military pageant and forget their disappointment.

The riding of the Marches is always a gala day in the burgh, and there are still living those who can remember the pagentry in 1830, 1852, 1873, and 1893. The latter was carried out on a scale of unexampled extent, and fittingly represented the industries, of which burgh and parish boasts.

The Coronation of Queen Victoria was celebrated with much enthusiasm and a profusion of floral decoration. The marriage of the Prince of Wales to Princess Alexandra of Denmark was made the occasion of a festal holiday, and to commemorate the event a couple of trees were planted in the shrubbery adjoining the south-east corner of the new stone bridge by Provost Riddock in presence of an immense concourse.

Her Majesty the Queen, the Prince Consort, the Prince of Wales, Duke of Edinburgh, and Duke of Connaught have all been to the parish. Her Majesty and the Prince Consort drove along the same old Mercat Gate along which many a former Scottish Sovereign had passed, and the three royal princes played golf upon the links. The Duke of Connaught was a guest at Carberry Tower and Pinkie House, and made an inspection of the Carberry coal workings during the time he was on duty with his troops at Piershill.

Among parish memories the Thanksgiving Service, held in Inveresk Church on Sunday, 26 June, 1887, in connection with Queen Victoria's Jubilee, will have an enduring place. Never before since its erection had the great church been so filled, and hundreds unable to gain admission remained outside on that lovely summer day. In that service Presbyterian and Episcopalian joined, for the time differences were forgotten, and Churchman and Dissenter united as fellow-subjects in offering praise and prayer to Him by whom kings reign, for blessings which they in common had enjoyed.

Chapter XXI.

DISTINGUISHED PARISHIONERS.

IN the long honour-roll of illustrious names which Inveresk can claim as hers by birth, residence, proprietorship, or service, those connected with Pinkie her oldest residential manor may be given the precedence. Following the days when Abbots of lordly line sojourned in it came keepers of the royal conscience,—lord high chancellors of the kingdom,—whose names have been already mentioned and of whose services notice has been taken. To it the Marquis of Tweddale entered in 1688, and in 1778 it passed by purchase into the possession of Sir Arch. Hope of Craighall, in whose family it continues. Sir Archibald's son, Sir John, was a conspicuous public man. When King George IV. visited Scotland, in 1822, the Archer Guard was put upon the same footing as the Life Guards in England, and Sir John Hope, Brigadier-General, was in constant attendance upon his Majesty whenever the guard was on duty. At Holyrood the Captain-General delivered the reddendo required by the Archer's Charter to the king,—a pair of barbed arrows,—

and at this function were present Sir John Hope and Admiral Sir David Milne, G.C.B., Inveresk, a member of the Council of the Body Guard. His Majesty conferred certain privileges on the Archers about this time, and presented to them a Gold Stick for the Captain General. The Duke of Buccleuch, holder of that office, had accordingly, as Gold Stick of Scotland, a place at the coronation of William IV. next to that assigned to the Gold Stick of England. The newly crowned king forwarded to the Royal Company a Gold and a Silver Stick, which, on their presentation, were carried by Sir John Hope and Sir David Milne, the next in command to the Duke of Buccleuch and the Earl of Dalhousie.

Sir John Hope was convener of the County of Mid-Lothian, and represented it in Parliament. He was Lieut.-Colonel of the Mid-Lothian Yeomanry Cavalry, and so popular with the regiment he was presented with his portrait, an engraving of which was published. Sir John took a warm interest in burghal and parochial affairs, and had a term of office as Town Councillor and Provost of Musselburgh. His son, Sir Archibald, in like manner served the community.

Carberry Tower takes rank next after Pinkie in point of antiquity. The date of its original erection appears uncertain, but it bears all the evidence of having been erected as a stronghold when "might was right." The tower, which two or three centuries ago would be regarded as a considerable family residence, forms now the entrance hall to the commodious and elegant mansion built in connection with it, and the upper portion having been most appropriately transformed into a splendidly equipped armoury gives an air of romance to its loop-holed walls. The bartizan is embellished with winged cherubs,—emblems of the spirit world,—antique mouldings, and surmounted by flagstaff and beacon-fire basket. The Laird of Carberrie, at the date of the battle of Pinkie, was one of four to whom the rejected overtures of Somerset were made known, and is otherwise notable. From this Hugh Rig's descendants, the estate passed into the family of Dickson and then into that of the present noble owner's ancestor, Fullerton of Carberry. In Wilson's Tales of the Borders a story entitled, "The Lost Heir of Elphinstone" appeared. An old lady, who remembers its first publication, associates the incidents of this tale with Musselburgh, and affirms that the heroine of the story was a comely fisher-lass, whom the waylaid heir returned after hardships and wanderings to claim and wed. As it appears in later editions, the scene is laid on the coast of Berwickshire, and the incidents are also altered, but this is in well understood keeping with the artifices of novel writing. The tale is attributed to "the happy dominie of the happy days at Abbotsford," the tutor in Sir Walter Scott's family. The villas of Inveresk have been possessed by Earls of Sutherland, Lord Eskgrove, Admiral Sir David Milne, the hero of Algiers; Horne Dalrymple Elphinstone of Logie Elphinstone, Sir David Wedderburn, Colonel Spence, Colonel Hughes, Major Yule, H.E.I.C.S.; Major Horsburgh, Lady Baird, Lady Milne, Lady Mary Oswald, Mrs. Admiral Home, etc. Pinkieburn was the residence of the genial Rev. John Watson, first secretary of the Congregational Union of Scotland, and later of the Rev. Wm. Lindsay Alexander, D.D., widely known for his accurate scholarship and his ability as a preacher. He was one of the Speaker's company of revisers of Holy Scriptures. Inveresk House was occupied early in the century by the Hon. Mr. Charteris, afterwards Earl of Wemyss; and Drummore by Lord Drummore, who endeavoured to introduce wool spinning as a local industry. Lord Stair, the distinguished jurist; Lord Haddington, Lord Clive, the Hon. North Dalrymple, Sir Ralph Abercrombie, General James Stirling, and many more had their residences in the parish. Monkton is said to have been built by the famous General Monk, and to have been so named by him. Early in the thirties, in a plain substantial dwelling-house in Eskside, between Bridge Street and Hercus Loan, an exciseman of

DISTINGUISHED PARISHIONERS.

the name of Fergusson lived. He had a son, Willie, who, when in attendance at Edinburgh University as a medical student, did the journey daily on foot. That young man became Sir William Fergusson, Bart., Serjeant-Surgeon to the Queen and the head of the surgical profession in Great Britain.

By birth, Inveresk claims Burnet and Walker engravers of the highest repute—the one in historic subjects, the other in portraiture; Handasyde Ritchie, a sculptor known to fame; David Macbeth Moir, poet and novelist. Among those distinguished in life, educated at Musselburgh Grammar School, may be mentioned Logan, the poet; Lieut. Drummond, who invented the lights known by his name, and who is understood to have been the draughtsman of the Reform Bill of 1832; and Mr. David Milne Home, who did much to promote scientific study, to popularise meteorology, and make it a means of forecasting coming weather.

On the inscription in the Churchyard the names of many who shed a lustre round them may be read. Numerous were the heroes of the Peninsular War who came here to die; and when the war was over, many a gallant soldier found a pleasant society and an agreeable retreat where the ploughshare turned the sods that once were drenched with human blood.

Colonel Sir Henry Yule, K.C.S.I., C.B., LL.D.,

R.E., is another distinguished Inveresk man. His father served in the Hon. East India Company's Service, and was sometime the British Resident at Lucknow. He was born 1 May 1820, at Catherine Lodge, where he remained till twelve years old. He entered Addiscombe Military College in 1837 and left it the following year at the top of the list. Appointed to the Engineers he received his training at Chatham before proceeding to India. His career there was a brilliant one, of the most varied service, untiring literary labour and unobtrusive benevolence. By successive Governor-Generals he was entrusted with duties demanding the utmost determination and resource and sent on important embassies to native courts. On his death, in 1889, the Royal Geographical Society and the Royal Asiatic Society paid high compliments to his memory. He was President of the Geographical Section of the British Association at its Edinburgh meeting, 1871, and received from the Royal Geographical Society "The Founder's Medal," 1872. He was a member of the Council of State for India, and had the degree of LL.D. conferred upon him at the Tercentenary of Edinburgh University. He was President of the Royal Asiatic Society, a Knight Companion of the Star of India, and a Corresponding Member of the Institute of France.

Of such a son Inveresk, surely, may well be proud.

Examples of New Communion Plate.

The parish is the birth-place of fishing-net making by machinery. James Paterson, a retired Commissariat officer, settled in the place, often observed with pity the fisher-folks employed in working nets for their husbands' use. He, being of a mechanical turn, perseveringly applied himself to produce a machine for net making. In this he succeeded, and soon found a growing demand for the produce of his looms. By improvements afterwards introduced defects were remedied and every diversified requirement met, so that from the factory by the Esk the fisheries of the world draw supplies.

A relic of Old St. Michael's, rescued from the oblivion to which it was consigned when the present church was built, has been again placed in a position where it can be seen. It is a monument to the memory of the Duke of Lauderdale. The inscription, in Roman capitals, reads :—

ILLUSTRISSIMUS.
Et nobilissimus princeps ac dominus
D Ioannes Dux de Lauderdale
Marchio de March Comes de Lauderdale et Guilford
Vicecomes Maitland dominus de Thirlestane
Musselburgh, Boltoun et Petersham
Sæpius ad parliamenta et ordinum hujus Regni conventus tenenda
Pro Rex
A restauratione regiæ majestatis per 20 annos
Solus pro regno Scotiæ regum optimo
Carolo 2do a secretis
Præses secreti consilii
Prædicto potentissimo regi in regno Angliæ a secretiorib . . . consiliis
Et ex cubiculariis primariis unus
In Scotia ex quatuor senatoribus collegii juridici extraordinariis unus

Castelli regii Edinburgeni constabularius et gubernator
Nobilissimi ordinis garterij eques natus 21 Maii 1616 Lidingtoni
Obiit 24 Augusti 1682 prope fontes de Tunbridge.
Unde corpus 27 ejusdem mensis delatum ad suum de Hamhouse palatium
In parochia de Petersham et comitatu Surriæ in Anglia
In suo ibidem sacello in 16 Octobris diem requievit
Exinde sua Scapha comitante regio Navithalamo
Ad Dounes secundo flumine advectum excepit regia navis præsidiaria
Que continuo ad portum de Fishcraw in Forthæ estuario ipsum trajectum
In hoc suo templo Musselburgen a 25 Octobris ad 5 Aprilis diem permansit
Quo die post funebrem orationem ab Ioanne Episcopo Edinburgen habitam
Magno cum splendore stipantibus regni proceribus
Clero et pene innumeris omnium ordinum hominibus
Hadinam translatum fuit ubi cum eximia et nobili majorum serie
In spe beatæ resurrectionis conditur
Justa et omnem exequiarum pompam
Summa observantia et pietate curabat
Carolus comes de Lauderdale
Frater unicus et successor,
Posuit. W.S.

This inscription may be rendered this:—

The most illustrious and most noble Prince and Lord Duke John, Duke of Lauderdale, Marquis of March, Earl of Lauderdale and Guildford, Viscount Maitland, Lord of Thirlestane, Musselburgh, Boltoun and Petersham. He very frequently held meetings of parliament and of the estates of this realm on behalf of the king. From the restoration from exile of his royal majesty Charles II. he was, through twenty years, the alone Regent for the Kingdom of Scotland. He was president of the Privy Council in Scotland, and was also a member of the Privy Council of England and one of the lords of the bed-chamber. He was one of the four extraordinary Senators of the College of Justice in Scotland, Constable and Governor of the royal

Castle of Edinburgh, and a Knight of the most noble Order of the Garter.

Born at Lidington 21st May 1616, he died 24th August 1682 near Tunbridge Wells, whence on the 27th of the same month his body was borne to his own palace at Hamhouse in the parish of Petersham, county of Surrey, England. It lay there in his own chapel till the 16th day of October. Thence his remains were conveyed down the river on board his own barge, which had a royal convoy, as far as the Downs. A royal guardship there received the remains, and the voyage was continued to the Port of Fisherrow, in the estuary of the Forth. His body lay in his own church at Musselburgh from 25th October to 5th April, on which day, after a funeral oration by John, Bishop of Edinburgh, it was removed to Haddington, accompanied by the nobles of the kingdom, the clergy, and an innumerable procession of all ranks. There it lies, along with the distinguished and noble line of his ancestors, in the hope of a blessed resurrection.

All the customary ceremonial of a great State funeral was observed, and it was carried out with the greatest care and dutifulness by Charles, Earl of Lauderdale, his only brother and successor.

W. S. placed this.

In this memorial to one of the foremost of the statesmen and Court favourites of his day we have proclaimed the prominence of the Duke's position and the honours that he received. Seldom is a greater contrast found than between the estimate here met with and the woful tale of his character and career which tradition and history have handed down. But, widely as these portraits of him differ, the particulars given in this inscription is of considerable value, for it shows the better features of the man—features which those for and with whom he acted doubtless admired, while those to whom he was opposed only experienced the severity of his rule and the harshness of his measures. Imperious in disposition, and with unbridled power at command, he was ill-fitted to understand those who were willing to endure in God's cause and to suffer death for Christ's sake. Of him it may be said he was a servitor of his sovereign, a suitor for self, but no good friend to his native land.

Along with other distinguished parishioners one lady must not be forgotten to be mentioned. In the list of heritors entitled to sittings in the parish church the name of the Countess of Hyndford appears. United by marriage to one of Scotland's illustrious families, her ladyship was linked no less to those old-world times when the elite of the aristocracy had their town-houses in the closes of the Canongate and Cowgate, and when the latter was a fashionable suburb of the metropolis. This

Countess was Janet Grant, daughter and heiress of Lord Prestongrange, one of the "crême de la crême" of Edinburgh society, when linkmen and Sedan chairs were indispensable, and when Hyndford's Close was witness to many a gay gathering.

Chapter XXII.

MISCELLANEA.

BY Charter, Musselburgh acquired the right to have "a mercat cross" and a free fair at the festival of Saint James. The cross is erected over a draw-well, and in local parlance is known as the Cross-well. It consists of a square building, with an upright shaft surmounted by a lion upholding the burgh shield. In all likelihood it has stood in its present position in front of the Municipal Buildings since its first erection. In those good old days when George the Third was king, a bonfire was kindled beside it on his Majesty's birthday, and the bailies and council came forth to drink the sovereign's health in public. This done with all the honours, the glasses used were tossed among the faggots that no other health might be drunk out of them thereafter.

In olden time Musselburgh Fair was of more than local consequence and considerable trade was done at it. It was considered the correct thing for a lad to buy his sweetheart "a stand of ribbons"—whatever that might be. But many a transaction of greater value was concluded. Cloth, boots, shoes, salted beef, and things substantial generally were the staple articles dealt in. A curious proof of this is met with in a Session Minute where several of the elders intimate they could not attend any meeting as they would be engaged at the fair.

Within the present reign the Lord Provost and Magistrates of the city attended the Edinburgh Race meetings on Musselburgh links in state. To the Fair Races, the Provost, Bailies and Council of the Honest Toun marched in procession to the rat-tat of the town's drummer.

By the Act of the Scottish Parliament, 1661, cap. C.L. entitled, *Ratification* in Favors of the *Toun of Mussilburgh*, the Baillies, Councill, Communitie and inhabitants thairof are confirmed in all their ancient "priviledges," "And siclyk ane act of the Convention of Burrowes holden at Stirline upon the third day of July 1618, Whereby the said Convention Grants and gives their license and tollerance to the inhabitants of the toun of Mussilburgh and ffisherow which shall be actual ordinar residenters therein with their houses and families, to resort to the tack of herring, salmond or white fish in all the parts of the Realme ; And their to pack and peill the same peaceably untroubled or molested be the said burrowes or their agent for the same."

The privilege thus acquired has ever since been

exercised by a brave and hardy portion of the parishioners. One of this class was for some years a member of the Town Council. At an interview with the late Duke of Buccleuch, this worthy, having on occasion supplied Dalkeith House, introduced himself thus:—"Duke ma' lord, I'm yére fisher." This was not the only representative from Fisherrow his grace encountered. A fishwife had been plying her calling among the villas at Eskbank, and at the gate of one of these was left with no one at hand to help her on with her burden. Seeing a gentleman approach she accosted him, "Eh! sir, gie me a help up wi' ma' creel," which was good humouredly done and for which she returned her thanks. She was shortly overtaken by another who enquired whether she knew who had given her the lift; "no me," was the reply. That was the Duke of Buccleuch, said her questioner. His surprise may be imagined at her ready wit when with outstretched hand she rejoined, "Can't be possible; see a shillin' tae drink his health." Such characteristic modes of expression are fast disappearing before modern habits, What would be thought now of a small shopkeeper-body holding conversation with a wholesaler in this wise. The humble dealer complains of the difficulty in getting accounts paid, and is brusquely told, "why do you trust these poor devils." "That's easy explained sir," says his in no way timid customer, "rich deevils like you wad never think o' dealin' wi' the like o' me."

Conventionalism robs us of the healthy frankness and sense of humour our fathers cultivated and indulged in. It is told of the weavers' society having at their head (annual) meetings adopted a rule to attend in black clothes and white ties. When it was first observed one of their number lifted the "sneck" of the door, peeped in, and exclaimed, as if conscious of having made a mistake, "losh! its the presbytery!"

Among distinctively local usages may be noticed Pie Monday. This is the Monday immediately preceding Dalkeith October Hiring-Fair, when everybody is supposed to have a hot mutton pie to supper. The custom is said to have its origin in this way. A baker who was on his way to the next day's market with a supply of pies was unfortunate enough to have his horse so lamed that he could proceed no further than Musselburgh, and cleared out his stock on terms favourable to the purchasers. The pies proved of good quality, and the next October he found the demand so brisk that his stock was exhausted, and he found it suit his purpose to cater for his Musselburgh customers as the day came round.

The Musselburgh Silver Arrow, shot for by the Royal Company of Archers, dates back to 1603, if not earlier. It is the oldest trophy of the Queen's Body Guard for Scotland, and has been more frequently won by noblemen than any other prize. The shooting for it was made the occasion of an imposing march out from Holyrood to Musselburgh in 1724, when the Duke of Hamilton, K.T., was Captain-General.

One of the divisions of the burgh in the seventeenth century was known as "God speed a.'" Of it incidental notice is taken in a Session Minute. It was situate between Market Street and Hercus Loan, about halfway between Eskside and Campie Lane.

The Mid-Lothian Yeomanry Cavalry was formed in 1797, and its mess meetings at Musselburgh were looked upon as social gatherings of no ordinary kind. It is said many gentlemen joined the corps, and others came from distant parts of Scotland for the purpose of being permitted to share in them. Sir Walter Scott, as quartermaster of the Edinburgh Light Horse, took up his residence at Musselburgh during the term of training. It is related of him that in the intervals of drill upon Portobello Sands he was often observed to retire to the edge of the water and walk his charger backwards and forwards, then, putting his spurs to her sides, dash off as at the charge. On his way back to Musselburgh he rode up to one of his friends and recited the stanzas of "Marmion," which he had been then composing. At one drill he received a kick from a Yeoman's horse which confined him to his quarters for three days. During that enforced seclusion Sir Walter employed himself upon the poem, and put "Marmion" nearly into the form in which it appeared. Of Tytler, the historian, Sir Archibald Allison tells that he was the very spirit of these mess dinners, and was wont to sing songs at them, recounting the incidents of the day's drill in the most grotesque and humourous manner.

Campbell, the poet of the "Pleasures of Hope," and Galt, the novelist, were likewise for a time stars in the society of the parish.

In the Notes to the "Antiquary" and to his Poetical Works Sir Walter Scott has a number of references to the locality, and some of his characters are understood to have had their originals here.

A curious minute of the Kirk Session of 29 January 1712 is illustrative of the condition of the period. "Testificats appointed to the bleu gowns in this paroch. To Peter Campbell, an ample and full certificate: to Robert Jackson, to Jas. Watson, a blind man; to Richard Robertson in Whitehill and his wife, Janet Robertson; and Thomas Craig." These were Edie Ochiltrees' of long before "the "Antiquary" was written.

As a glimpse of how things were managed under the close corporation system, the following copy of the invitation issued for the Michaelmas

Dinner in honour of the privilege which the Council enjoyed of self-election is given; the name of the invited being for personal reasons withheld.

The Magistrates and Council present compliments to———beg the favour of his company to Dine with them in the Townhall on *friday* next, the 29th inst., at 3 o'clock.

Musselburgh,
September 1797.

The form is printed from an engraved plate, the word Friday and the figures 97 being all that is written.

Copy of Burgess Ticket given for placing the Weather-Cock upon the Town Steeple, 1654:—

"The Sextene day of November
Jaj vi^c and fiftie-four yeires.

The qlk day in presence of Robert Strachane, ane of the Baillies of the burgh of Mussilburgh, and in presence of Sundrie of the Counselleres personallie convenet for the tyme, Compeired personallie William Craig, eldest lawfull sone to burghs George Craig, Seaman indwellar in ffisherow, and is maid a burges and frieman of the said burgh of Mussilburghe, and he gave his oath of fidelitie conforme to the order, and payet for his friedome and burgeship to Martene Robertsone, present thesaurer of the sd. burghs. The soume of Sextene pundes Scots modifiet be the Baillies and Counsell in respect that some of the Counselleres did affirme that the said George Craig did put up the Widdercock boone the *point* of the knokhous, and it was at that tyme promist and agrret be the Baillies and Counsell to mak him a burges and frieman for Undertaking such a haizard and doing such a piece of Service to the good town. Extract be me George Vallange, clerk of the said burgh.

G. VALLANGE."

The Act of the Scottish Parliament Charles II., Cap. C.L., 1661, from which extract has been already made, is a Charter of Confirmation of " All and whatsumever Charter," etc. the town of Musselburgh had previously obtained, and particularly that granted by " umq^{ll} " Robert Comendator of Dunfermling with the consent of the convent thairof for the tyme." It enacts further "also his Maiestie with consent forsaid hes of new given granted and disponed to the said burgh Baillies, Communitie and Inhabitants thairof all and haill the samen burgh of Mussilburgh, ground and lands thairof within the bounds and limits vsed and wont conprehending the touns of westpans, fisherrow, Newbiging and others lyand within the territorie of the said burgh. With power and priviledge to the saids Baillies as Baillies to his Matie (Majesty) and his successours to receave resignations and to grant infeftments, . ·. . And with power to create burgesses sua far as may be compitent to ane burgh of Barronie or Regality, And with power likewise to the saids Baillies, Councill and Community to labour and manure such pairts and portions of their Comonty as they shall think expedient to the well and vtility of the said burgh, . . . With power also to the saids baillies, Council and Community to creat and make yeerly at Michaelmas two bailies, Thesaurer, Officers and all other members of Court needfell for administration of iustice within the bounds foresaids," . . .

By virtue of these extensive powers the Magistrates of Musselburgh had, and still possess, the right to confer the freedom of the burgh upon such as they think worthy of that high compliment, a right which parliamentary burghs have not had conferred upon them. Hence when a large community like Leith for example, wishes to acknowledge conspicious public services it may present an Address, but cannot make the recipient of it a burgess and freeman of the town, as old chartered burghs can.

Until the exclusive right of burgesses and guildsmen to trade in towns was abolished, to be a freeman burgess conferred a substantial privilege. So highly was it valued that, when the difficulty to find men to fill up the regiments and man the fleet during the wars with Napoleon was most severely felt, the right to carry on trade in any town upon obtaining discharge was a bait used to induce enlistment, and that came to be extended so that the sons and grandsons of soldiers could claim it likewise.

It was reckoned the duty of the magistracy to see that a sufficient number of the different tradesmen required in a community were maintained, and in this way they regulated the constitution and government of trade guilds.

Those of Edinburgh in the fifteenth century fixed the price at which claret was to be retailed by the pint, and the present writer has seen the forms used in much more recent times by the bailies of Musselburgh to say what was to be charged for bread within the burgh.

In the Chartularies of Musselburgh the Rules of the following trades are recorded in full:— Websters, Baxters, Taylors, Cordiners, Shoemakers and Tanners, Wrights, Seamen and Mariners, and Gardeners.

These Rules, having been approved and confirmed by the Council, provided that any dispute arising under them was to be disposed of finally by the bailies or one of them.

An extract or two may be taken as illustrative of the spirit and scope of the whole. Those for the Gardeners provide for example by

Rule 1. There shall no man of this society break the Sabbath day, or be found drunk, or breaking and abusing any of the Lord's most Holy Laws, under the penalty of twenty pounds Scots money.

Rule 6. That no person being ane unfreeman of this burgh or not of this society shall presume or be permitted to take a yard or yards within the libertys of this burgh by himself or an unfree servant to be hired by him for that effect above the yearly rent of   Scots until first he makes himself burgess and enter to our Society under the penalty of ten pounds Scots, to be disposed of by the bailies, and that each Incumbent to the burgh who did not serve his apprenticeship to any of our Society shall pay to the box at his entry four merks Scots by and abune making himself a burgess, under the penaltie of being fined at the bailie's pleasure.

Rule 11th provides that if any gentleman pay the Society £12, 12s. Scots his name would be recorded in the Society's books and he would be entitled to a plant of every kind any member had provided such member had not fewer than three of the same.

Rule 12. That there shall be none of our Society curse nor swear nor upraid nor abuse his brother in public or in private, penalty 12s. Scots for each transgression.

Rule 22. All Indentures, etc. to be written out

BIT OF OLD FISHERROW.

by the Town Clerk, penalty double fees *Toites Quoites*.

About Education the Bailies and Council had a great care. Frequent entries deal with the appointment and dismissal of schoolmasters. One minute declares a school to be vacant because the attendance of scholars had so much fallen away from the "bad attendance of the present maister;" another under circumstances which are thus explained. "26 Sept. 1720 Petition made by Mr. John Williamson (? the parish minister) and upwards of fourtie others inhabitant burgesses that the English School in Musselburgh and under the administration of Mr. William Keith as maister is gone entirely to ruin there being not one scholar at the school at present, as is also evident to the Council, they therefore declare the school vacant and allow any well-qualified person to petition for the office of schoolmaster for Musselburgh."

Immediately this is done the vacancy is filled up the same day. The Council having instantly received petition from Thomas Young, burgess of the burgh of Musselburgh for being received as English Schoolmaster and being satisfied of his sufficiency they do admit and receive him as English Schoolmaster in place of the foresaid Mr. Wm. Keith during the pleasure of the Council allenarly, he by acceptance of said office to be obliged to quit his present employment of tanner-trade with all expedition."

The Bailies and Council not only appointed the Schoolmasters, but the school boys many a time looked to them for what they considered as even more important service, and were as a rule not disappointed. When some good excuse was forthcoming to petition for a holiday, or even a half-holiday, grave was the confabulation held till a deputation was chosen to interview some tender-hearted city father. One lovingly remembered in this connection was Alexander Vernor of Holmes, provost of the burgh. Not only did the "laddies" get their petition granted, but frequently their pockets were filled with fruit by the provost's good lady.

This game was played to some purpose during the great frost in the spring of 1838, when the Esk was frozen from the damhead to the lower ford for six weeks without a break. Curling and skating were enjoyed to the full, and so thick and strong did the ice become that carts and horses crossed upon it. So far into the season this spell extended that the rector at length declared against any further half holidays, even if the frost should hold till mid-summer.

In the year 1850 the Town Council of Musselburgh found themselves in a dilemma. The inhabitants had begun to crave for better cleaned and lighted streets, for more efficient watching, and to rouse themselves to tackle improvements. Many a tough tussle the councillors had over the expense of keeping a lamp here and there lighted from dusk till dawn. The fight was in the first place over lamps at doctors' and bankers' doors. Gradually better thoughts prevailed, and it came to be acknowledged that a well lighted town gave thieves and burglars fewer opportunities to ply their calling. This, of course, meant increased expenditure, but the voters always voted against the imposition of any assessment. The annual balances were as a consequence on the wrong side, and the needful was obtained by taking loans on bills at one day's date, but even this did not always suffice. At last the pinch came, and the creditors impatient. One of them took diligence upon an unpaid bill, and a messenger-at-arms arrived in town with instructions to put the law in force. He accosted the provost—Provost William Campbell—and told him either to find the money due or go with him to jail. The provost did not relish going to the Calton alone, and obtained respite on undertaking to summon "an important meeting of the Council on urgent business" for the evening. To this the unsuspecting bailies and councillors responded, but as each entered the Council Chamber click went the lock of the door to his astonishment and dismay. An agent for the holder of the bill was present and put before them the two alternatives of being taken off to imprisonment or consenting to his being appointed judicial factor for the burgh. To the latter alternative they unwillingly agreed, but by application on their behalf to the Court of Session it was set aside. This crisis led to the "Estate Act" being obtained from Parliament in 1851, under which the Common Good was administered by Trustees representative of the Creditors and Council. Unable any longer to apply the income from the Common Good to such purposes as lighting, cleaning, watching, the ratepayers were compelled to submit to being assessed, and thus relieved of a drain it was unable to meet, the Trust Estate gradually recovered, and the Trustees had the satisfaction to restore the administration of the town's property to the Town Council seven years ago.

So late as in Delta's time, the Town's Common was of such extent as to furnish grazing for a hundred cows, and the burgh had a town's herd to look after those of the burgesses which fed upon it. This functionary blew his horn in the streets in the morning, and cow after cow in answer to its call came forth to join in the departing herd, and in the evening upon their return from browsing,.each "fell out of the ranks" as it approached the entrance to its own byre.

On the border of this old Common two shepherds'

houses stood, back to the era of the Battle of Pinkie. A reminder of them continues in Shepherd House at the point where the Carberry and West Mains roads separate in the village of Inveresk. The other of these two is beside Pinkiehill dairy, and has in former times consisted of two flats, the under one some steps below the surrounding surface level. Most probably these two shepherds' houses would be an appendage to the houses of the Newbattle monks close at hand. The enclosure wall of Inveresk Lodge bears evidence of great antiquity and marks the direction taken by the old road to Newbattle as shewn in Blaeu's Atlas.

During the body-snatching period Inveresk Churchyard had an evil reputation for the desecration of graves, and a determination to punish the perpetrators led to an outbreak of popular fury for which the town had to pay the piper. A party bent on rifling a late buried coffin drove up to the entrance gateway. A party of watchers scared them and the gig in which they had come was left when they escaped. The hue and cry raised soon spread and when the gig was brought into the town, the horse was unyoked, ropes had, the gig set fire to, and it was dragged through the principal streets, brought back to the Cross and there smashed, that it might wholly be consumed. A survivor of the scene is the boy who ran to the "smiddy" for a hammer to help break it up. The gig proved to have been a hired one and the hirer unaware of any illegal use to which it was to be put. He therefore claimed damages for the destruction of his property and was successful.

On the two handsome stone pillars at the east entrance to High Street, Musselburgh, the burgh shield and 1770 are placed. That indicates a period of enlightened local administration. The midraw with the Chapel of St. James had been cleared away, and the mail coach road had been diverted from the old bridge through High Street. The Council had prohibited new houses from being covered with thatch, ordained the gutters to be causewayed, prevented the slaughter of cattle upon the public street, and made some further sensible sanitary regulations when these were enacted.

Over the entrance to the old prison is an appropriate inscription in black letter on white marble, and upon the lintel of the Manse Lane entrance to the minister's house, "I am a stranger on the earth," in Hebrew characters, much weather worn. The appearance of the stone indicates it is very old, and it may, with considerable probability, be thought possibly a lintel of the old vicarage.

INDEX.

	Page.		Page.
Ax	2	Bannatyne Club	86
Agriculture	8	Beltym	86
Antiquarian Museum	12, 42, 46	Blackhall, Rev. A.	86
Agricola, Julius	20, 27	Blackhall, Mr. A.	97
Advocates' Library	26	Blackhall, Jean	113
Anglic Invasion	31	Black, Rev. Alex.	186
Aneurin	82, 34	Branks used	131
Auld Brig	36, 68, 70, et seq.	Beggars' Badges	144
Antiquarian Soc. Trans.	44	Burnt House, Collection for	132
Altar. Appollina	45	Burgh Charter	221
Art and Religion	52		
Ancient Taxatio	60	Carberry 2, 4, 10, 19, 45, et seq.	
Alexander, Prince	61	Carlyle, Rev. A., D.D.	
Annuell of Mussilburgh	67	4, 7, 9, 38 et, seq.	
Act against Golf and Football	76	Cedars of Lebanon	8
		Craigmillar 9, 10, 113, et seq.	
Alhallowmes	77	Cists found	13
Archdeanery of Lothian	89	Cromwell, Oliver	9, 43, 124
Archbishops received at Musselburgh	156	Colony, Early	14
		Coal Formation	17, 18, 19
Archers, Royal Company of	203	Cowpits	18
Accounts, who to audit	152	Caesar, Julius	20
Approach to Church, North	165	Cold Hill	23
Absence of Delinquencies	166	Catraeth	33, 44
Alarm, False	199	Carella	36
		Colt, Robert	41
Buccleuch, Duke of	8	Caledonia Romana	41, 43
Bronze Period	13	Cardonnell, Adam	47
Britain	20, et seq.	Craigentinny	48
Beveridge, Rev. J. G.		Chalmers Caledonia	48
	18, 46, 189, et seq.	Communion, not observed	64
Bodotria	22	Colt, Adam	88, et seq.
Bede	25, 53, 55	Colt, Oliver	122
Bellesheim Alphonse	29, 62	Colts of that Ilk	98
Bedford, Earl of	44	Crown and Kirk	101
Brunstane	47, 83, 123	Cousland	87, 114, 133
Baptist, Feast of John the	61	Communion Cups	118
Bruce, Robert the	67, 71	Carmichael, Rev. Fred	168, 174
Binnock, Binning	69	Church Seats	129, 166
Bannockburn	71	Coalhewers	131
Burnt Candlemas	74	Christening Feast Forbidden	140
Bailies before Parliament	79		
Build that house to the skies	80	Collections Plundered	142
Baird, Inspector	80	Colleague, Question of	161
Burne, Rev. John	84	Communion Collections	138

232 INDEX.

	Page.
Church, reading in	141
Church-Bell, Ringing of, at Funerals	144
Collection by the "Brod"	144
Corn Purchased in England for Poor	172
Council Apprehended	227
Dalkeith	1, 7, 47, 84, 89
Drummore	6
Dunfermline	54, 55, 58, 59, et seq.
Denarius of Trajan	46
Delta House	46
David I.	59, 69
De Berwick, Robert	60, 73
De Bernham, Bishop	61, 64
De Pinkeny, Robert	67, 68
Dunbar, Earl of	68
David II.	74
Dutch Trade	75
Dials, New Town Clock	76
Duthie or Douchtie	82
Diurnal of Remarkable Occurrents	82
Dambrae	84
Dunfermline, Earl of	90, 101
Dickson, Sir Robert	161
Dun, Rev. Wm.	161
Droopsey	153
Distinguished Parishioners	201
Esk	1, 2, 3, et seq.
Ex	2
Esce	2
Escemuth	2, 55
Edinburgh	10, 33, et seq.
Eidyn	33, 34
Early English	34
Ecclesiastical Buildings	57
Ethelred	59
Edward, Flight of	71
Endowment Granted	77
Edinburgh University	92
Elders Admitted	141
Elders Resign	172
Estate Act, 1851	228
Firth of Forth	1, 22, 27, 55
Fields Enclosed	8
Fa'side	10, 46, et seq.
Fife	11, 23
Forestry Exhibition	16
Frissian Immigrants	30, 31
Fisherrow	41, 47, et seq.

	Page.
Fofriffe	56
Faulan	60
Figgate Muir	68
Fawside, Thos., Kt.,	68
Fawside, Roger of	71
Froge, Bailie	79
Falkirk, Teind, Scheaves of	87
Forbes, Sir John	91
Firance, Parish	146, et seq.
Fast-day Indulgence	128
Foundation Stone of Church	183
Grammar School	113
Golf Green	4
Gindi	25
Germans	32, 34, 35
Gildas	32
Gododin	33, 35
Gaul	35
Gough's Camden	49
Gothic	54
Gregory IX.	60
Ghillie	70
Golf	75
Gordon, Sheriff	81
Gordon, Rev. Dr.	94
Gibsone, James	104
God Speed a'	218
Home, David Milne	6
Howe Mire	8
Hailes, Lord	26, 57, 58, et seq.
Haddington	31, 54, 61, et seq.
Hope, Sir John	37, 203
Hope, Sir Arch.	72
Hope, Sir J. D.	72
Hope, Sir Thos.	123
Hepburn, Lady Janet	38
Hypocaustum	40
"Honestas"	73
Hollanders	75
Hereford, Earl of	83
Haliecroce, Convent of	87
Hislop, Rev. Philip	88
Husband-lands	114, 116
Hamilton, Marquis of	124
Howieson, Rev. Mr.	159
Inveresk	1, 23, 27, 31, et. seq.
Innes, Thomas	26
Inveresk House	38, 41, 42, et seq.
Inveresk Gate	41
Inveresk Lodge	94

INDEX. 233

	Page.
Ive de Addeburgh	54
James, King	59
Inundation	75
Irvine Harbour	163
Imprisonment for Disobeying Session	134
Inchmartin, Parliament at	68
Jedburgh	23
Joppa	6
Jubilee Service	202
Kirk Park	12
King William	90
King Alexander II.	60
King William the Lion	61
King Alexander III.	67
King James V.	82
King James VI.	87, 90, et seq.
King Charles I.	124
Kolf	75
Kirk, Repair of	142
Kirk, Byding out of	133
Kirk, Bible, cost of	151
Kirking of Newly Married Couples	143
Kilmarnock	145
King's Birthday, Celebration of	214
Land, Rental of	8
Lowe, Bailie	12
Lowland Scotch	34
Lucius III.	60
Linlithgow	51, 54, 69
Lindisfarne	55
Laurie, Provost	80, 190
Loretto Chapel	81, 113
Leslie, Bishop	82
Lindsay, Sir David	82
Lauderdale, Earl	87
Lauderdale, Duke	123, 154
Leynes, Edward	86
Linkfield House	124
Musselburgh	1, 2, 21, 44, et seq.
Monkton	6, 114
Monktonhall	6, 18, 114
Magdalene Burn	1, 6
Mary Queen of Scots	10, 43, 45, 199
Magdalene Bridge	12
Midfield	18
Municipium	41

	Page.
Musselburgh Bailies	43
Manse	46, 84. 96, 103, 166
Malcolm Canmore	53, 55, et seq.
Manumission of Slaves	69
Mar, Earl of	73
Moodie, Beannie	81
Maitland, Chancellor	87, 94
Milne, Sir David	204
Milne, Sir Alex.	42, 46
Maitland Club	86
Millholme	95
Music School	96, 113
Middleton, Earl of	155
Millar, Rev. Arthur	159
Moodie, Rev. Leslie, D.D.	188
Marble Playing on Sunday	141
Monuments, Lauderdale	
Monuments, Mr. Smyth	158
Memorial against Proposed Presentee	168
Masonic Ceremony	182
Militia in Camp	185
M'Neill, Andrew	158
Michaelmas Dinner	219
Moir, D. M. Delta	24
Newton	1, 86, 87
Newcraighall	18
Newbigging	42, 145
Normans	54
Northumbria	55
Newbattle	67, 97, 145
Nidreth	73
Nairne, Duncan	93
Ox	2
Ouse	2
Ormiston	31, 68 83, et seq.
Odin	85
Orme	68
Oxingait	114, 116
Ordination Dinner	165
Prestonpans	1, 10, 126
Pinkieburn	6, 17, 18
Plough Improved	7
Pinkie, Battlefield of	8, 10, 46
Pinkie	67, 68, 90
Pinkie, Battle of	198
Prince Charlie	10
Prehistoric Remains	12
Pottery, Ancient	14
Parliament, Scottish	38
Patten's Expedition	46
Paris National Library	65

Q

INDEX.

	Page.
Preston of Craigmillar	76
Pasche	76
Pilgrimages	82
Paterson, Hist. of Regality	82
Pleuch-lands	114, 116
Parish Church, present	182
Psalme before Service	132
Pands	148
Parish School, Anent	161
Presentee proposed, objected to	168
Queen Mary's Treasurer's Book	44
Queen Margaret	56
Ravensburgh Burn	1
Romans 20, 23, et seq.	
Richard the Monk	25
Roman Bridge	35
Roman Bath	38
Roman Fort	38
Roman Urn	46
Roman Roads	47, 48
Roman State	47
Romanesque	54
Randolph, Earl of Moray	71, 72
Randolf, Abbe	71
Randolph's Lodgings	72
Restalrig	47, 91
Register of Ministers	86
Report on Parish, 1627	111
Records of Kirk-Session	127, et seq.
Riding of Marches	201
Royalty in Parish	202
Statistical Accounts	4, 18, 72
Sea Margin (old)	5
Silchester	36
Subterranean Passage	42
Somerset, Duke of	43, 46, 197
St. Mighael's	47
St. Michael's	49, 50, et seq.
St. Monenna	50, 51
Shire	54
Statute Labour	59
Smeaton	60
Stury, Simon	60, 73
Synod of Musselburgh	62, 65
Sacred Music	64
Stephen Eddi	64
Slaves in Scotland, English	70
Scott's Fasti	93
Session Minutes	96

	Page.
Stoneyhill	114
Sharp, Lord William	157
Smyth, William	158
Seats in Church Erected	166
Sundial, Manse Garden	173
Select Society, The	176
Sunday Schools Established	177
Stent on Musselburgh	122
Schoolmasters, Spoken to	134
Seamen's Loft	143
Stile, North	139
Stile, South	162
Sackcloth Used	132, 141, 162
Seats for Scholars	139
Sabbath Burdens, Carrying	140
Sutherland, Earls of	206
Society Rules	223
Tranent	1, 17
Trees, Ancient	16
Trade Followed Flag	20
Teutons	30, 22
Tynninghame	31, 55
Tolls, Exemption from	59
Town Clock	76
Tarres Croft	115
Tokens, Communion	135, et seq.
Usque	2
Usk	2
Urns Found	12, 13
Undresk	47
Vogrie	23
Vicar's Well	84
Vernor, Robert	160
Wallyford	18, 69
Walting Street	22, 47
Witenagemot	81
Woden	35
Water Supply	48
Wynton, Andro of	50, 61
William the Conqueror	58, 70
Wallace, Sir William	57, 68
Watch and Ward	73
Wishart, George	88
Whitchill	114
Whiteside	115
Westminster Assembly	154
Williamson, Rev. John	160
Weekly Sermon	134
Witchcraft Suspected	142
Walking on Sunday	165

www.ingramcontent.com/pod-product-compliance
Lightning Source LLC
Chambersburg PA
CBHW031252250426
43672CB00029BA/2182